HEALING FROM CHILDHOOD ABUSE
!WE HAVE A VOICE NOW!

Written and Illustrated by
Julie Martins's Miracle System
First Re-Print March 2002
Second Re-Print September 2002

Published by
Miracle System Press
Huntington Beach, California
June 2002

MY SIDES AND THEIR JOURNEY BACK TO LIFE

POEMS REFLECTING MY MANY LIVES

HEALING FROM CHILDHOOD ABUSE

!WE HAVE A VOICE NOW!

Written and Illustrated by
Julie Martins's Miracle System
First Re-Print March 2002
Second Re-Print September 2002

Published by
Miracle System Press
Huntington Beach, California
June 2002

MY SIDES AND THEIR JOURNEY BACK TO LIFE

POEMS REFLECTING MY MANY LIVES

ISBN 0-9702723-0-8 $20.00
Library of Congress Catalog Number 00-092018

Printed in the United States of America.
Copyright © 2000 by Julie Martin
First Re-Print March 2002.
Second Re-Print September 2002.
All rights reserved.

DEDICATION PAGE

This book is dedicated to three special people:

Tammy Ichinotsubo, Ph.D., who literally saved my life when strength was nearly gone after 13 years and 9 therapists who could not help me. I had come to believe I was *beyond help* and did not know how much more endless pain, terror, and despair I could bear.

Thank you for your kindness and warmth that brought me safety within to continue coming back. I was blessed with your ability to help me process memories, maintain boundaries, and amazingly not trigger me to leave. Thank you for your never-ending patience throughout each session. I am being put back together again--I can feel it. I'm healing. It's a miracle from God--the gift of Tammy.

Bobby Martin, my loving brother whose love and innocence brought safety within to love unconditionally. He gave me faith that I must be capable of love during many moments of my life when I doubted my capacity to love anyone. I always knew I loved him so just *maybe* I could love.

He has no idea how his precious face broke my heart and kept me alive during those darkest moments. My inability to find the words to say good-bye to him kept me here when pain had surpassed the threshold of toleration yet leaving him was not an option as I knew how much he depends on me and how much I love him.

Dan Halterman, for 10 years of unconditional love, loyalty, and placing value on me that I had never experienced before and needed more than he ever knew when expression was lost within. Through your unconditional love and loyalty, you taught me how to begin to receive love though I did not have enough internal safety or healing to give love consistently.

Thank you for always feeling my heart while I doubted its existence and acted out time after time. All the many times you called me your *Rough Tough Cream Puff* meant more than you knew to the mute inside with no voice who was so happy you felt her presence. I am sorry for all I never knew and all I could never be and all I was unable to give that only in healing I am beginning to see. Thank you for believing in me and some how understanding me when we neither had a clue but some how you knew. Thank you for fulfilling *widdle me's* dream of a papa for those 10 years. God bless you.

God, for filling me with faith, hope, and truth. Thank you for holding me near in those darkest moments. Your abundant love, power, presence, and words taught me I am lovable, valuable, and have a purpose.

ACKNOWLEDGMENTS

Benjamin Martin: You have no idea how much impact your words of encouragement had on me as these writings poured out of me, and I shared them with you. Your friendship and many hours of positive support gave me the gentle push and added strength to move forward with purpose and transform my life into an inspirational book for all to see. Thank you so much for allowing me to use your computer software to typeset my book to reflect each of my sides' lives to perfection. I will never forget how you laid on the floor in your office handing me page after page of print outs as we would chuckle at how they precisely emulated each story. I remember how in the "wee" hours of the night you would patiently wake to the "hum" of the printer to hand me yet another page all the while telling ME I needed sleep. We both came to know I was on an unstoppable mission two-plus-days straight until it was complete. Thank you for being there.

Sal Iniguez: My book would have been an impossible dream without the hard work, diligence, and many long nights I heard you spent shaping my first spiral-bound book into a reality that validated my life and gave me hope as an author. You went the extra mile perfecting the positioning of the words on each page never demanding exorbitant fees. It was obvious to me from the beginning that your motivation remains in your service and your great integrity to your work. One of the main reasons I continue to frequent "Copy 4 Less" is because of the kindness of the staff. And your dedication will always be remembered. Thank you.

Marti Richelli: First, I want to thank you for selecting me to live as one of four roommates in your safe, quiet home in Huntington Beach. In 1998, as my life went from bad to worse, I had a peaceful home and room where I could stop, feel, and heal. I am grateful for your patience with my "processing of pain" and respecting my need to be left alone. I had been graced with a healthy, safe haven where I could stop and begin intensive therapy. It comforted me knowing that you and Tracy were just a few steps away. Additionally, I appreciate your letting me spend many long hours on your computer in the garage as these writings escaped into print and eventually became my first book. Finally, I want to thank you for the gift of the computer so that I could continue to write and complete my second book "Facing Reality," which will be available in latter 2002.

Hossein Nader: Because of you and "Copy Run," I was able to get my book printed and out to the public without the volume that most printers require that I could not afford as a first-time author still in therapy twice a week healing from childhood abuse. I thank you for your faith in my book and your generosity of heart. With this first re-print, my book will fulfill previous and subsequent orders, replenish stock at the sold-out bookstore, and enable my book to become accessible to larger bookstores and the community as a whole. I look forward to continuing business with you. God be with you.

TABLE OF CONTENTS

PREFACE

What you are about to read are the personal stories of my *Sides* whose lives reflect the varying emotions that for years have been trapped inside my body, separate, with no expression until triggered out. Then, each *Side* became my life. As their voices came out of me (*"The Howl"*), I cried tears of relief as I realized what a miracle it is that I am still here. That was when an omniscient *knowing* came over me of how important and necessary it was that this book reach other survivors. I matter today; the darkness is gone to the extent I have known it (*"Doom"*). I have lived a lifetime of pain, shame, terror, and despair imprisoned within my body, mute, yet living out the chronic abuse of my childhood clueless while triggered emotional *Sides* expressed themselves left and right as I was continually thrown from present to past. I experienced panic attacks (*Terror*) as a child (*"Getting Scared"*). One day they just stopped. *Terror* came back in my early twenties as I went from doctors to therapists trying to find out what was wrong with me. For 13 years, I went to over 9 therapists and nobody could figure me out as I experienced never-ending pain, confusion, and symptoms. Through the years, I was diagnosed with Major Depression, Panic Disorder, Mood Disorder, Obsessive Compulsive Disorder, Borderline Personality Disorder, Generalized Anxiety Disorder, Chronic Post Traumatic Stress Disorder, Bi-Polar Disorder (*"Rapid Cycler"*), and Agoraphobia. I was given medications that did not work and/or did not consistently ease my pain or symptoms. I have lost more jobs than I can count. I have been unable to maintain friendships and/or healthy relationships [*"A Foreign World (Love)"*].

It was not until March 1998 that I found my now therapist, Tammy Ichinotsubo, Ph.D., who diagnosed me with a Dissociative Disorder. That was when the puzzle of my life began to go together. The diagnosis matched my symptoms — the baffling holes of my life began rapidly flashing back — I finally had renewed hope that maybe I could get better. I stopped and began over three-hour sessions of intensive therapy with her twice a week to this day. I am a walking miracle. In all honesty, the only reason I am still here today is because of my strong faith in God and my developmentally disabled brother who is 29 but has the mind of a very young child. He is unable to speak and was also abused. I could not leave him. I have come to believe that early enough childhood trauma can cause or enhance developmental delay, severe social or relational problems, and emotional and mental retardation as you seem to wither away or into a withdrawn shell inside your body that is characterized as you. Up until I was seven years old, I had no knowledge of what a world of light was. I lived in darkness. I never knew what a dream was. My sleep was filled with nightmares during those earliest years prior to our move to Cerritos at age seven where my family and I spent the next nine years. I believe at least *Cindy, Ju Ju, Margaret,* and *Sam* were present during that time before the move. It was not until recently (which in part resulted in a delay of this reprint) that I became aware of harrowing medical evidence of physical abuse and/or neglect that took place before I was five that ironically validates my memories. There is something sticking out of my neck to the left of my voice box that I had been told all my life was just part of my body that I recently found out is, in fact, a foreign body composed of some type of metal.

When my family and I moved to Cerritos, other *Sides* were born or came out as I went from darkness to light while those earliest *Sides* of me, I believe, became frozen or dormant somewhere inside as I was shielded from conscious awareness of their existence, yet their view unknowingly distorted my perceptions as their presence occupied my life. My world changed after our move to Cerritos. I knew the difference between darkness and light because I was not living in total darkness any longer. It became a far-off memory that always puzzled me. I believe *Sally* may have been developed during this time though she may or may not have been present to other people as much as to ourselves as she brought us confidence to the point of grandiosity, calm from the fear, and the illusion of freedom. Unfortunately, to this day, Sally mainly comes out, ironically, after tragedy. She represents our freedom. She has no fear but has never known how to be present when things are good. Usually, when things are good, *Sabotage* takes over. After that move to Cerritos, the horrible nightmares of death began to mingle with normal dreams that I had never known were possible, and I had thanked God for them. But within a year or two of moving to Cerritos, when I was around eight years old, the panic attacks began where I believe I lived in *Terror* at night with no memory but *Margaret's* shame in the morning.

I believe the holder of those younger, playful, innocent grade school years was *Sandy* whose memories I am, 30 years later, beginning to recall—my childhood. I lost many of *Sandy's* silly, playful, frivolous, spontaneous, impulsive ways when I disowned her deviously hysterical and possibly seductive nightly encounters with our grandfather. He was over daily and on many nights babysat my sister, our infant brother (after he was born when I was eight and a half), and myself. I believe *Sandy* owns our feelings of sexuality that we are now learning to claim in a healthy manner and which was greatly mirrored by the unconditional love and support of our ex-husband through 10 years together. *Sandy* would take over for *Margaret* and *Terror* during those childhood years. I believe when *Sandy* was out, we were all tucked away with no memory of her existence. In later life, we found words in our diary concerning her along with expressions, behaviors, and attitudes we had come to know were held by her alone. These include the good childhood memories that we are recalling in therapy.

Through many years of patterns and cycles ("*Insanity*"), I became co-conscious and began to refer to them as my *Sides*, my *moods*, how I *get*, and how I *act* not quite understanding what that meant since it was all I had ever known. My life is transparent now. Whenever I am in doubt, I just remind myself that I would be dead, but I am not dead. Consequently, it does not matter; I am not protecting anyone anymore; and nothing more can happen to me that has not already happened! The voices of dissociation imprisoned within me have broken through, been released, and are free to speak—ME—my emotions. If I had died, they would have been buried inside my body MUTE like my life. I have a voice now after all these years. Through my writings, you may find faith, hope, and inspiration. These poems may be the basis to facilitate processing of your own powerful emotions and the internal struggle and turmoil that such a battle of confliction involves while reassuring you that you are not alone and that you will survive if you DON'T GIVE UP! Paradoxically, at the bottom of the pit, the miracle happens.

INTRODUCTION

I am a survivor of chronic childhood abuse. Much of the abuse was deeply buried and forgotten. It by no means went away. The defenses of its manifestation kept the me I was born to be buried deep inside while my life became a performance, and I died (*"Role of a Lifetime"*). A lifetime of symptoms baffled and shamed me more: Pain, fear, anxiety, panic, depression, despair, and doom with associated moodiness, isolation, alienation, terror, and confusion. I received a high school diploma and college degree while simultaneously drifting through a lifetime of lost jobs. When childhood abuse makes feeling and existing at the same time impossible, survival takes over (*Veronica*). Especially at a young age when defense mechanisms and/or coping methods are minimal. I had to split off or separate from the truth as I knew it since its harsh reality and pain was too much to bear (*"From Life to Death"*). Since I lived in an atmosphere that I could not escape for years, the part of me that lives while another part of me is gone begins to become more than those dissociated emotions. What I have come to understand is that each *Side* began to have its own life separate from mine, which I did not always know about. Since there were many triggering elements of abuse and neglect in my life, I split off from various feeling emotions that I was inherently born with as a whole. The longer the abuse continued—and certain feelings lived compartmentalized in me only coming out to survive—the more those emotions also became separate from me each living their life or functioning through me (*"Life Compartmentalized"*). I made it through childhood alive in body but a maze of split identities and confusion reside inside that I was clueless to even after I was away from the unsafe environment of home and going about life in my late teens. Insanity began as my life became a chaotic web of confusion similar to childhood but now acting out of me as an adult. I now believe that as a child and young adult I may have been less aware of my *switching* with very little consciousness to my life since I have very little childhood memories at all. What I thought were my memories for years were pictures I had seen from family photo albums or that I had watched re-play on movie projectors. And as an adult, how do you comprehend or articulate when you are trapped within the maze of your destined internal system without a clue of what is happening to you (*"Maze of Dissociation*[1]*"*)!!??

First of all, I was living most my latter childhood as a detached, walking dead, anorexic-appearing zombie/host we call *Veronica* who took over for *Margaret* and/or *Sally* more often since *Sandy* disappeared for some time after early childhood. *Vicky* came out often in late high school years with a trip into a more likable bundle of energy (*Joe*) during the first few years of college. No wonder the doctors thought I may be bi-polar/manic depressive!! *Joe* went away more often as I became seriously involved in my first intimate relationship with Dan, who became my husband and partner for over 10 years. His love brought out *Cindy* whose twin *Sandy* was accepted lovingly. Dan loved *Veronica*, understood *Vicky* (*"Love Turned to Hate"*), and was gentle with *Margaret* (*"Lost Life"*) who came out frequently too. However, the shameful, fearful *Margaret*, who wished only to be invisible (*"An Unsafe World"*), mingled with the panic attacks of *Terror* resulting in our desperate search for help. I did not know at the time that I was dissociating. I just wanted to be back the way I only remembered being, which was happy, friendly, and vivacious *Joe* who was coming out less often! During my college years, I had begun to believe I was *Joe*. And *Margaret* vaguely reminded me of a clouded past life I

---

[1] You will find in second book entitled Facing Reality, ISBN 0-9702723-1-6 (available in latter 2002).

forgot I knew that I did not wish to recall. I was considered *moody* all my life and my perceptions of the world and people around me kept changing. (As more years went by without proper diagnosis, I came to depend on the *switches* to counter the suicidal yearnings after years of consistent inconsistency.) I had come to realize that since I was still here, I knew how to survive—I have been good at that—without even knowing that I was surviving as I had been doing it so long. But once I had come out of the danger zone of my home life, flat-lined *Veronica* stepped aside and, *Uh Oh*, I began to feel (*"From Flat-Lined to Feeling"*). But, you see, that is when the real problems developed and life became utterly unbearable. Everything feeling inside of me (my *Sides*) was detached from what I had come to know as me (*Joe*) and held buried memories of what I forgot I knew. It is my understanding that my love and trust of Dan brought out Cindy whose love touched the need that had been deeply buried [*"The Need (Unconditional Love)"*]. This stirred up much chaos among the *little ones* (*"Love Without Desperate Need"*).

So as Dan and I began our life together in 1986, my symptoms increased as everywhere I would go and everything I would see and all that I would do in the present triggered a feeling *Side* of me—that was extremely wounded and that I had disowned—who came out to survive the past it knew while I had no clue as each *Side* lived through me (*"Clueless Existence"*)! The dilemma is that what triggered that emotion out had to do with something usually not dangerous in the present but rather in some subtle—but huge—way reminded that *Side* of a past that I did not even know was triggered!! Except, now I was gone until I came back wondering what was wrong with me!! My *Sides* have looked after me and have behaved in ways to protect me not knowing I do not need protection anymore. My life began to unravel and become completely out of control as the confliction of my survival self, host, or walking dead (*Veronica*) is trying to mask or cope with the ambiguity of my internal system that I do not even consciously know exists. I thought I was just *fine* until I started jumping out of my skin left and right with escalating panic attacks and Terror while losing jobs because of *attitude problems* and *personality conflicts*. The last thing I remembered, I felt fond of someone, who I then began behaving ambivalently toward like an *around-the-world* yo-yo on its own course. So, I began to learn that when I *feel*, people trigger a not so *society acceptable Side* out (*Vicky*). And if I stay to myself to keep a job, I began to discern through the years from comments made, lack of popularity, patterns, and *co-consciousness* that I had become *anal* (*Rose*). I did not like this, but she became necessary for me to function at work at all. (*Rose* may have also been present and considered *the boss* at bedtime back in childhood when we would compulsively arrange to sleep with at least a half dozen stuffed animals.) I had tried working at large companies where I would be invisible, but all the people triggered me. So, I tried working at smaller offices where there were less people only to find that they would want to get to *know* me which caused further difficulties. I even began taking temporary jobs. That way, by the time I got to know the people, my assignment was over. But the stress and inconsistency caused anxiety too especially when wherever I would go, people would *want* to get to know me. And as much as I did too, I came to know better.

In approximately 1993, I found one job that I kept longer than most because somehow I trusted a female co-worker who seemed to understand how I *get*. She was sometimes able to reach and pull me out of my distrusting cycle of mind distortions (*"Mind Distortions²"*) so I did

---

² You will find in second book entitled Facing Reality, ISBN 0-9702723-1-6 (available in latter 2002).

not *switch* as often or begin the wild, endless internal shuffle through my *Sides* while I am gone to the present and am instead lost somewhere inside my head (*Ju Ju*). (Through years of therapy, I have come to realize how often I have been gone not understanding my time lost until I gain consciousness to voids of moments past as I receive glimpses into others' bafflement and my confusion.) Besides, at this same job I mentioned, my boss liked me, respected me, and seemed to accept me just the way I was on any given day. That permission—that freedom—and positive validation made all the difference in the world though he wound up an *enemy* too as *Vicky* told him off for all his kindness that she perceived was ultimately against us!? But, because at that point I was working a strong sobriety program, I was able to make amends and release some of the self-hate that consistently flowed through me like lava. Of course, I simultaneously managed to *work-a-holic* my way out of the office parties at work. When that was not possible, sometimes the *little ones* came out and the boss expected me to go back to work afterward not understanding that, that was not in their plans, and the day was shot. How could I explain that to the boss—let alone myself—when I did not understand somewhere inside why I was acting certain ways and my vocabulary, math abilities, office skills, computer knowledge, comprehension, memory, perceptions, normal routine, and sometimes close-up vision seemed to change unpredictably as years went by. I came to realize that some days the computer-strain glasses seemed to be blurry, but I must have been imagining it! Another baffling, confusing hole to add to my own internal belief that I must be *crazy*. I have been hearing voices since I was a child that terrified me until I must have managed to deny their existence so I could pretend I was sane. As an adult, I came to believe that it must be a result of my undiagnosed Schizophrenia that I would rather not know I have. (Amazingly, that was one diagnosis that the doctors had never given me yet I had constantly given myself.) It was not until Tammy, my now therapist, told me that Schizophrenics hear voices outside of their heads—not inside their heads—that I was given a hint of hope from insanity.

As years went by, I began to comprehend that I JUST CANNOT FEEL since my behavior became quite unpredictable and I was *moody* all over the place while I never knew how or who I would be. Insanity had taken over my life as I came to know my *Sides* who I, conversely, had no control of while I witnessed myself *bouncing around* or *switching* with varying comprehension and glimpses of consciousness at limited times. During those most difficult years, as we struggled to continue working, *Rose* took over in order for us to keep a job for any length of time, which continued to decrease through the years. At home, I lived anxiety day in and day out (*"Anxiety Attack"*) or depression that after years became isolation, alienation, and despair (*"Weighed Down by Depression"*). The fear-free, self-confident, and independent *Sally* would come out as we neared each brink of catastrophe in our lives, jobs, and in our marriage. She would sustain us through the rough moments but then go away. Sometimes we would cycle back to *Margaret* who would undoubtedly surprise the people we were or had most recently been in contact with and further humiliate us as we became aware of our inconsistency. The excitable people person *Joe* seemed to be gone regularly. However, after we separated from and subsequently divorced our husband, we began to notice that she would make more appearances when she was around older men or felt the approval of other men. This seemed to sustain her and replenish her life. She is called *kiddo* often and appears to be in her early teens. She loves to have fun especially in the company of a *father figure*. Through the years, *Sam* was consistently out more often making our life unbearable and daily running necessary. By that time, I almost wished I could feel the unbearable *Terror* again that made me an agoraphobic by day and a drunk by night (before sobriety) just so I could know I was alive. But some how I made *Terror* go away—just like in childhood! I became so tired of the endless darkness of *Sam* that had become my only life, since *Terror* was gone, WHILE I ATTEMPTED TO NOW SURVIVE MY ADULT LIFE!!! Sometimes we would find ourselves curled in a ball on our favorite spot on the bathroom floor where we would enter the land of a more pleasant nothingness. When that void was more than we could bear, *Ju Ju* began to burn or cut us just so we could feel something. There were times when feelings I was not aware I buried became conscious—and at some level I grasp existed—but I knew that I must keep them buried at all costs as they equal death. Yet life without feeling IS death, but I had forgotten this until *"The Howl"* because I had been dead for so long. YOU MUST WALK THROUGH THE DARKNESS OF STRONG DENIAL TO EVEN GAIN ACCESS TO THE TRUTH YOUR SYSTEM BURIED (*"Miracle System"*). That same system deeply believed my knowing its reality was detrimental to my survival (*"Are My Sides Sabotage or Protection?"*). So, I had spent my life living DEAD in the dark projecting them cluelessly—yet sabotaging ME—because, of course, my worth was a reflection of all I was taught through the hate and shame transferred to me that became my own belief back when I died and their false reality became my life (*"Sabotage"*)!

I spent years seeking many therapists, being given many prescribed drugs and diagnoses, listening to self-improvement, affirmation, and relaxation tapes, and reading many self-help books trying to understand and feel better yet nothing really worked. My life had become a repetitive cycle of endless pain that made no sense (*"State of Confusion"*). Years of sobriety and working a strong program had taught me acceptance of my *Sides* I had come to know so I could at least stop hating myself so much. By this time, I had lived a great deal of my time in anger, rage, and self-hatred that I projected out to the world (*Vicky*). As I began to learn self-love, *Vicky* came out less. I was sometimes able to be kind although I felt awful. *Vicky* was becoming tamed. I made it my goal to become a good, loving, and giving person. Amazingly, I learned that when I connected to being a good, loving, and giving person, the pain went away quicker. I found short cuts or avenues where I could *switch* more quickly into a more pleasant *Side*. I found post-it notes all over the bedroom and bathroom mirrors in my home reminding me to feel *no matter the terror!* The steps of Alcoholics Anonymous have facilitated the healing process for me more than any previous therapist. I asked God to remove my character defects while I contemplated that these may in fact be my *Sides*! Since pain was always present, any delay to that pain was desirable. I became willing and trusted that God knew what He was doing. I came to believe that He would not remove any vital part of me. (At the time of this re-print, miraculously, I have over 11 years sobriety.) Hence, through my growing relationship with God (*"Developing a Relationship With God"*), I began to desire change for less selfish reasons.

In 1997, a wise, loving adult seemed to be born or developed from within me and began to come out often (*JWK*). Yet, I would still cycle to and fro and was unable to be consistently *fun loving, fluid Joe* or *spiritual, all knowing JWK* or *confident, free Sally*. Instead, I was just beginning to gain more clarity into the reality of my internal catastrophe! I was hopelessly spun within the deepest layers of my intricately designed spider-webbed entrapment while I began rapidly fluxuating to the point of lost and hopeless entanglement. Somewhere inside a *Watcher* could only witness the confusion below as like an *Energizer Bunny* my life went chaotically from *Side* to *Side* with no direction and under the control of triggers from a past whose doors remained shut to our consciousness to keep us from remembering. There was a time when I believed I was beyond help—way too messed up for even the doctors to fix. Deep inside (mute), I had glimpses of all the *fear* and *shame* (*Margaret*) and *bad* (*Sandy*) that I must hide. I thought to myself that I had better accept one of those diagnoses that did not quite put the pieces of the puzzle together and made me feel crazier as I consecutively contemplated medications that did not work except for the one that NUMBED ME OUT MOST THE TIME. But, then, if I took that, I would remain as dead as my internal system had already made possible, and I would end up a statistic with all hope gone as darkness would finally completely seep over. The only life I had ever known was unendurable, but as I approached death—where for years I fantasized its reality to get through another day—I experienced glimpses of eternal hell ("*Hell*") and realized I needed life. Death did not appear to be an option either—now I can't even die!

In early 1998, by the grace of God, I found Tammy Ichinotsubo, Ph.D., a psychologist whose face I found warmth. She specializes in childhood trauma. I was referred to her through someone from a survivor meeting (that I avoided for years although by now I had been to just about every other conference, workshop, twelve step meeting, and support group that existed trying to ease my pain and symptoms). Early on, Tammy gave me a homework assignment that turned into an eleven-hour nonstop project—plus a few straggler hours. She asked me to draw my *Sides* that I was *always talking about*. I never really understood how well I knew them until I did that assignment—which a partially reduced portion became the front cover of this book. She told me about dissociation which I had come to contemplate with much back and forth denial. It was the one diagnosis that made sense, though, as my whole life began to flash through my head and misunderstandings, confusion, and memories filled in the holes of my baffled mind once I moved beyond the *label* and understood what dissociation really meant for me. I was diagnosed with *Dissociative Disorder Not Otherwise Specified* in conjunction with *Chronic Post Traumatic Stress Disorder*, which I had previously been diagnosed with at least two other times.

In November 1999, when once again I did not feel I could bear the pain and darkness any longer as I sunk deeper into the black hole abyss ("*Hell*"), God came into my room in light and saved my life ("*Saved By God's Light*[3]," an expounded "*God's Presence.*") Miraculously, I was saved and did not die. Shortly afterward, an enormous eruption of pain burst from my body ("*The Howl*") during an anger release (*rage*) meeting, my whole life changed, and this first book was created. I believe this book is my voice many years later. All the trapped, buried, and wounded *Sides* that have lived in my body mute for years (my emotions) are being set free. That was when I began to FEEL LIFE and FREEDOM ("*Freedom*"). They now have a voice. I have a voice. I am coming alive! I broke through denial, the darkness went away, and I matter again. I have begun to put the pieces of the puzzle of my broken self back together, which helped once I had a diagnosis to facilitate comprehension and Tammy to assist me in keeping track of how I behave. I have come to learn about myself by witnessing my trapped *Sides* out where I have become more present to hear them, look at them, understand them, and process the feelings that come out as a result of them. My life has been an insanity cycle of *switching* and painful emotions that made living impossible. I may still *switch*, but I am also becoming more *present* and aware of my *switches*. I can sometimes bring myself out of a less favorable *Side* or process thru and cycle back into another *Side*. I also know that each

---

[3] You will find in second book entitled Facing Reality, ISBN 0-9702723-1-6 (available in latter 2002).

emotional side is not all of me NO MATTER HOW MUCH IT FEELS LIKE IT. I do not *switch* as often, which has THANKFULLY decreased the *pinball* and/or *ping-pong ball* effect of living. Some of the most unbearable and endless feelings of pain and despair have been reduced to a degree I never dreamed possible. I have begun to understand why others want to live. I believe therapy with Tammy and possibly Divine Light and timing brought me to *"The Howl,"* which is responsible for the development of this book and my miraculous survival. That was when I began to remember *like in a far-off dream* what it was like to feel again (*"Fluid Emotions"*).

I recently spiraled through another rough patch in recovery. Regrettably, I continue to suffer grave emotional distress, isolation, and social alienation co-mingled with healing as I continue to walk through memories so that I may be put back together again (*"Healing"*). I learn about my life and me as I heal. And I hold on to my faith and the truth that my life is coming together. I am being reconstructed no matter how torn apart I feel at times. I am reclaiming my lost selves. Slowly, but rest assuredly, everything is happening in just the right timing. I pray that some day I will have people in my life. People happen to be my biggest trigger, and they are everywhere! Such stimuli are usually avoided by my *Miracle System* so that my life flows more smoothly. Sadly, people unintentionally compound this when they become afraid of my diagnosis since they are unaware of what it truly means. They only have *movies* and *hype* to guide their intuitions. I am the same way I have always been except now I have a diagnosis and map to expedite my healing. We who dissociate to the degree I do are just wounded human beings trying to function in this world while constantly being tossed into our past world because of childhood abuse that was not our fault in the first place! Only in healing do I realize to the extent I have lived in the past and acted out because of where that past sent me all the while having *no clue* that *you* just became *them* as my *"Miracle System"* frantically flees or makes you leave.

Simplified, if people could just think of my *Sides* as nothing more than their own emotions that come out freely as they feel and when they choose. Unfortunately, I have never had control of my emotions—since other people controlled them. I had to adapt or die. So, as a child, my emotions split off from me as a whole numerous times so that I could adapt. As each *Side* came out to survive, and years went by, each then grew into their own life. Then, through years of becoming aware of my *Sides* and getting to know my *Sides*, I became co-conscious of them (*"Becoming Co-Conscious"*). Consequently, through much pain, shame, panic, confusion, struggles, and despair, I came to accept them, which was necessary so that I could learn to love myself. And through such acceptance comes possibility for change since you cannot change what you deny. Through much therapy came further knowledge, awareness, communication, and understanding as to what made them split from my core in the first place. We also work at cooperation among them so that I have more control of my life and more balance to how I spend my time while I learn to manage my behavior by becoming aware who is out and why they have come out so that I may process and heal that portion of my *Side*. Sometimes I can be the *Side* that is necessary in a particular situation of my life through cooperation among my *Sides*. This leads to more stability and control of my life. I believe the names of my *Sides* happened automatically through the years as a way to identify who was out or try to remain sane among the inconsistencies of my selves as I became co-conscious. This helps in differentiating who is doing what and working at having the appropriate *Side* deal with the situation they are most gifted at handling. And in therapy it helps the integration process when we can identify each and every one of my *Sides* and their origin so I can eventually become whole. So although our behavior may be unpredictable and inconsistent at times, we are also honest in every given moment and desire human relationships with other people who can accept the full scope of human emotions that we exhibit since we have no longer disowned our feelings. Ironically, so many *Singletons* have repressed certain emotions of their own to the point our purity of emotions trigger their disowned reflections that they wish not to acknowledge and face in themselves. Unfortunately, as a result of this, and their fear, some people avoid us once we tell them about our dissociation when we are the ones in therapy willing to walk through our wounds and become as whole and healthy as possible. I humbly believe that I have quite a bit of understanding into other people and am more together than many people as a result. There is a certain degree of wisdom that comes with being broken to the point that I have been. Togetherness breeds hindsight and knowledge into human emotional development as I witness my own reconstruction.

Since I did not die, I have something powerful, inspiring, and necessary to say. Hospitals, doctors, therapists, and people need to know that dissociation is not as isolated as we once thought. Dissociation runs along a continuum scale, and I know there are many who dissociate like me out there quite possibly being misdiagnosed. They may know themselves by their birth name but have no control of their life. I do not want anyone to have to go through the pain, struggles, and confusion of living with an undiagnosed Dissociative Disorder. So many of us are abused. So many men I have spoken with tell me that they have known, dated, or married a woman who had symptoms like mine (*"Mirror Image of an Incest Survivor"*). That is because abuse is widespread especially among women. And all survivors dissociate! Dissociation is not a mental illness; it is an intelligent, creative way a child survives the agony of their childhood. So, creatively splitting off to survive such trauma and betrayal is not only smart but also necessary. The problem is that when you become an adult, it does not just go away. That is where the insanity begins. Therapists need to know what it looks like. My experience of that is depicted in *Dissociated Life* and *Maze of Dissociation*[4].

I realize that I am no stronger than any other survivor. I truly believe that besides the all-merciful grace of God, my handicapped brother kept me here longer than most can tolerate it to the point my life will make a difference. I made it beyond the point of no return from darkness and back to the light. I believe others may recognize themselves through me, sustain hope, and find the necessary therapy to heal from the devastating effects of childhood abuse and the possible symptoms of dissociation that without a voice they will be unable to articulate until it may be too late. In being *present* more often in each fluid moment I begin to find out what living is—what *being* is (*"Being"*). I finally understand what *being present* means as I begin to experience this (*"Transformation"*). For years, I have been either in my past or my future to the point I knew no other life. Now as I catch glimpses of *being present*, I savor them (*"Living in the Present"*). And when I come back from being gone, I become thankful for the times I am *present* once again. As I experience living *present*, life becomes good. When I go away, somewhere inside the *Watcher* remembers. I have renewed hope that I will be *present* again now that I know what that looks like. I have tasted living, desire it, and understand as I heal, I will gratefully experience it more often.

---

4 You will find in second book entitled Facing Reality, ISBN 0-9702723-1-6 (available in latter 2002).

Now, at moments, I gain access to my fragile core who is beginning to incorporate these sides into me. I have witnessed her growth from what felt like a raw, naked baby coming out of a sheltered seed. I have felt a powerful foundation of strength and safety stemming from this most deep level of me that is beyond words yet can only mean that the most damaged, wounded, and broken parts of my being are mendable. I know this because I am living it. The core of me is reincorporating all my sides at such a fundamental level, which is a miracle that escapes words, but rather proves the incredibly awesome possibilities we as human beings have to mend our souls through God, therapy, willingness, and perseverance. All my life I have felt unsafe and have looked for safety outside of me not even understanding what that meant. Now I can feel my core warmly enveloping me with this incredible base of safety I never received as a child.

All the while, the love that is *Cindy*, who has been encapsulated within me mute most my life, is becoming safe enough to peak out, blossom, and grow within me as I experience her presence at times. She is a most loving, caring, and feeling human being who likes being out but has never had control of her time out. She has been held hostage, imprisoned but protected within, for way too many years as we now become safe enough to let her venture out and into this world more often. I have come to believe that Cindy is the holder of the deepest levels of our love. I have felt her, in essence, growing up to new levels of maturity. Some of the pain that has always accompanied her existence has been released (*"Umbilical Cord Release"*). She is able to connect with and care about other people on a human level apart from the spiritual love of *JWK*. However, relationships are very difficult. As we develop more safety within, my *Miracle System* will allow Cindy to be present more often without interference. Since we spend most our time with ourselves, we have come to know our true goodness and heart, as we are not projecting the past onto someone else and mistaking that for who we are. Some day, we will be able to share who we have come to know exists with trusted people we allow into our life. This has become possible through much therapy and positive mirror reflection of a couple trusted people (and our *Ginny*) who still remain close to us. Unfortunately, since our trust has been terribly shattered (*"Shattered Trust"*), nearly everyone else triggers the insanity cycle as we *ride the tornado* of recovery that makes it, ironically, healthier to abstain from the human race altogether. We look forward to the day we can see the world consistently through lenses of today and love people with a heart that has so much to give.

When I am able to see the world as *JWK*, relationships flow more smoothly (*"Co-Dependency Cure"*). Her spirituality and understanding of divine truth makes all betrayal and hurt dissolve. She sees way beyond human error (*"Reflecting Christ"*). Sometimes I wish to see the world as she does consistently. Such truth brings more freedom and love than can possibly be described. When you experience God's love, you can love without fear in immeasurable, unspeakable ways. This brings much peace, joy, and bliss (*"God's Love"*). I am grateful for her teachings and wisdom and the knowledge that she lives within me. As I heal, I am beginning to look at wholeness as having access to all my feelings all the time—not to live in just one but to move from one into the other fluidly without hindrance—to be safe enough to live. It is a never-ending process of walking through the old, facing the present, and then letting it all go so you can enjoy each day anew (*"Breaking Free"*). I have found that it is very important that you find a trusted therapist since all the insight in the world was not making me better on my own. Alone, I could not get outside of and beyond my triggered *Sides* in order to process and own their reality. The only way out is to walk through each and every wounded part of you. Each area you wish not to touch will just hinder your life that much more. One major lesson I have learned is to always face and let go of today all that I feel because whatever you ignore, avoid, deny, repress, escape, disown, or dissociate from will never go away. Some day you will have to face and walk through layers of it when carrying it around finally knocks you down. Let it go today; do not delay inevitable pain you will have to face some day that will further *taint* and limit your life until you do. I believe you must communicate, share, write, hit, cry, scream, and GET THAT PAIN OUT OF YOUR BODY. It is amazing how your body remembers and stores it, and WE CARRY IT AROUND. That release may expedite the healing process by breaking through the denial. When I heard the inhumane animal-like sounds catapult from my body during *"The Howl,"* any last doubt of the devastation of abuse went away. You will find buried underneath those most internalized, unimaginable nightmares of your unworthiness, a most beautiful, loving creation [*"The Paradox (Walking Through Darkness Brings Light)"*]. You will realize there is a compassionate, understandable reason for all those deep-seated fears of your *badness* that once processed, on the contrary, conveys wisdom of your inherent goodness and value, which breeds deeper levels of self-love (*"Cycle Back to Love"*).

When those repressed emotions no longer live inside of me, the depression just vanishes naturally. It has been my experience that medications do not help—they only mask—what I am too afraid to face and may only result in a delay of healing. At times, however, medications may be necessary to keep me from hurting myself through those most difficult times as I prepare myself to face another level of feelings I have longed to escape. But even more so for me, running maintains my serotonin levels (without sedating my *Sides* who finally have a voice), keeps me strong and helps me face, walk through, and conquer just about anything. As I begin feeling, communicating, and taking action concerning conflicts with the reality of my personal power each day, depression can no longer occupy my space. When I behave and communicate with honesty and integrity, and then let it go—and give it to Him—no matter the outcome, all is okay exactly as it is. Depression lives in oppressed, repressed, unexpressed, and hence powerless emotions. Once the performance stops, and we are free to just *be*, our true essence of life shines through and anxiety dissipates. We have our power back, we have our voice again, and we have our life back! We are no longer lost inside imprisoned in endless darkness or a statistic who died as *crazy. They* become exposed—our shame dissolves—we become free (*"Freedom From the Shame of Fear"*). Over four years later, still in intensive therapy, I can feel the indescribable, unmentionable, impossible knot untangling like thread unwinding as layers become exposed and released and free from the tightly wound spool they were trapped beneath—closed and locked doors that concealed me. I know that some day I am going to be whole. And that is one unbelievable miracle of God and the gift of Tammy.

SHATTERED
TRUST

WHEN TRUST IS SHATTERED,

    THERE IS NOWHERE TO GO.

EVERYONE IS THE ENEMY;

    FRIENDS AND FOE.

DESTROYED AND BROKEN, CONFUSED AND DISTRAUGHT;

    THERE IS NOWHERE TO GO—HOW DO YOU RUN FROM YOURSELF?

THEY PLAY WITH YOUR BRAIN; THEY PLAY WITH YOUR HEART;

    'TILL NOTHING IS LEFT BUT TO SPLIT APART.

NO ONE CAN HURT YOU;

    YOU ARE ALREADY GONE.

JUST PUT BACK TOGETHER: AN IMAGE OF GOODNESS; A LOOK OF KINDNESS;

    A MIND OF NOTHINGNESS OR SHEER HATRED AND CRAZINESS.

SURVIVING AND BLENDING INTO THE CROWD;

    DEPTHS OF DARKNESS SO DEEP.

NO ONE CAN REACH THROUGH THE DEPTHS OF DESPAIR AND MISTRUST—

    INSANITY CREATED FROM INNOCENCE.

FOR TO REACH THAT PRECIOUS CHILD,

    YOU MUST ENTER THE WILD:

THE PAIN AND DECEIT, DISTORTIONS AND BETRAYAL,

    LONELINESS AND HELPLESSNESS, HATRED AND RAGE.

UNSEEN EYES JUST WAITING TO KILL THE MOTHER FUCKERS

    FOR MAKING ME DIE.

I'VE WORKED A LIFETIME ON LEARNING TO LIVE:

    TO BE NORMAL, TO BE LOVABLE, TO BE WORTHY, TO BE GIVING—

TO BE ALL THAT I'M NOT.

    ALL THAT WAS TAKEN! ALL THAT YOU GOT!

1

I HATE YOU! I HATE YOU!

  YOU TOOK ME AWAY.

LEFT ME WITH FRAGMENTS CLOSED OFF FROM MYSELF

  WITH NOTHING TO FEEL AND NOWHERE TO GO.

DOORS SHUT TO THE CLOSENESS WE TRULY DESIRE.

  SUCH FEAR AND PARANOIA--KNOWING WELL WHAT YOU TAUGHT.

SO, NOT A CARE IN THE WORLD

  BUT TO TRY TO LOOK GOOD, FIT IN, AND GET BY.

TRY TO BE NORMAL, TRY NOT TO LIE,

  TRY TO FEEL GOOD WHEN YOU'RE EMPTY INSIDE.

TRY TO LEARN LOVE, KINDNESS, CARE, AND TRUST

  WHEN BENEATH THE SURFACE THERE'S SQUISHED BLOODY GUTS.

SHATTERED AND BROKEN AND THROWN AWAY

NOTHING SOLID, DEPENDABLE, OR TRUSTWORTHY IN WHICH TO STAY.

  EMPTINESS SPINNING IN SPACE.

JUST TRYING TO LEARN HOW TO FIT IN A WORLD

  WHEN YOU'RE SO UNDONE AND FEEL LIKE YOU HAVE NO ONE.

GOD CAN REPAIR EVEN THE DARKEST OF SOULS

  WHEN DEATH BECOMES DESIRABLE TO THE LIFE YOU KNOW.

SURRENDER AND GIVE HIM YOUR LIFE

  AND WHAT'S LEFT OF YOUR HEART.

HE HAS TAKEN MINE UNDER HIS CARE

  WHEN THERE IS NOWHERE TO GO; JUST UTTER DESPAIR.

MOMENTS OF FREEDOM AND HOPE AND LIGHT

  AS CLOUDS PART IN RECOVERY, AND I BEGIN TO HEAL.

AS THE DARKNESS BEGINS TO FADE,

  AND I REALIZE MY LIFE HAS BEEN CLEARLY BLOWN AWAY.

I BEGIN TO SEE WITH NEW EYES--A NEW LIFE--

  AND FEEL THINGS A DIFFERENT WAY.

I GRIEVE FOR ALL I'VE NEVER KNOWN,

AND OTHERS HAD ALL ALONG.

THEIR FOREIGN WORLD—MY EYES RECEIVE FLASHES.

I BEGIN TO DREAM: CAN I REALLY GO ON? CAN I REALLY GET BETTER?

CAN LIFE BE WORTHWHILE? CAN I BECOME FREE?

FREE FROM THE ONLY LIFE I'VE EVER KNOWN . . .

HIDDEN AWAY WHERE NO ONE COULD SEE . . .

JUST LAYERS BELOW THE IMAGE OF ME.

GRACE OF GOD

By the Grace of God, we survived that world;
By the Grace of God, we didn't give up.

By the Grace of God, we desired a soul;
By the Grace of God, we didn't give up.

By the Grace of God, we were brought humanness;
By the Grace of God, we didn't give up.

Although we struggled and failed;
By the Grace of God, we didn't give up.

So many times, we teetered near death; but
By the Grace of God, we didn't give up.

By the Grace of God, we feel our strength and His love;
By the Grace of God, we didn't give up.

By the Grace of God, we hunger for love;
By the Grace of God, we didn't give up.

By the Grace of God, we feel love;
By the Grace of God, we didn't give up.

By the Grace of God, we see our darkness;
By the Grace of God, we continue to look.

By the Grace of God, we long for connection;
By the Grace of God, we didn't give up.

By the Grace of God, we begin to feel the oneness;
By the Grace of God, we didn't give up.

By the Grace of God, we yearn to trust
In an inner world that just never got;
By the Grace of God, we don't give up.

By the Grace of God, we remember our past--that hell;
By the Grace of God, we don't give up.

By the Grace of God, we understand our life; and
All that we had to be and all that we've become.
By the Grace of God, we're still here.

By the Grace of God, we begin to feel NEED;
By the Grace of God, it doesn't kill me.

SOUL CONNECTION

To love so deeply, so purely; two souls connected. Time stops, blissful eternity--so warm, so true, so safe. Each touch so gentle; eyes reaching beyond, mesmerized by each others' souls. Thoughts unspoken, dreams made; feelings over-flowing too deep for words. All expressed in just a gaze, a touch. Two eyes knowing, penetrating. Love like never before. . . . So awesome, so indescribable. Each soul speaking words unheard. Time passes--yet doesn't exist.

I know you, I really know you. I recognize you. I love you. You're my soul mate. You've reached through the depths of me. Your goodness has found mine, and it is a sacred place no one may share. It is our space, and no one will ever know it. The place we go in each others' embrace. The depths of tenderness, love, and knowing. Bliss we experience in each others' eyes.

It seems I've gone back in time--back to God's love before the world made me forget. Where my body became separate and my spirit became ruled by my ego. Where time exists, and people and sin and hate prevail. Yet all along and for a moment I knew . . . God is love and I am love and you are love and love is eternal and I experienced that blissful knowing with and through you.

We are so lucky, so fortunate, so naked, so true. We opened our hearts--vulnerability seeping through. Hearts so fragile yet so secure; so exposed, yet so safe. Two souls knowing the truth--the love. The gift was opened; D-J World was reached. No fear where love so pure runs through two souls no longer distant--two bodies no longer separate. The connection made, the oneness felt, the love divine. The center of me reached the center of you. Where no ego, no fear, no games exist. Just purity, love, truth, bliss.

We experienced that world; that I'll always treasure. I pray I may again live that knowing where for a time it all made sense. All was safe, and there was no such thing as fear. That world of freedom before the insanity of the mind began to take its toll.

Each touch so special, so meaningful--so necessary. What if it stops? What was once so beautiful is now so terrifying. What if he goes away? That look, that embrace, that kiss. What if he strays? Where does unconditional become conditional? When do you start counting what you can give by how much you get--got to keep track, keep score, be safe, hold back?

The point where your heart cries out: I'll do anything. . . . you begin doing nothing. The moment your hands not tire of touching his body, you go paralyzed when he's in your body. The moment your heart feels terror at a night apart, you take a week apart. The moment you vision him in your future, an actual glimpse of you two in your future, hope and terror strike evenly.

Don't tell him you love him, let him tell you.
Don't let him know you, he'll only hurt you.
Don't reach for his hand, he'll just reject you.
Don't hold him in your arms, he'll withdraw from you.
Don't give him your heart, he'll betray you.
Don't tell him you need him, it'll kill you.

Hope dashes--you must run, get away, dare you live another day.

Just go through the motions of everyday life. Distant and smiling, no connection, no life. Not feeling--just pretending everything's alright. Coasting, no thrill--just endless hours--suffering, trudging, recovering, accepting--yet lacking our true spirit's desire. Always yearning for the day where I may be healthy enough and you willing enough that we may say: *I love you, you love me, please never go away.*

But even if you do, my heart is strong enough, my mind is well enough, and I am whole enough for two souls to connect once again and for all I ever wanted to finally come true: I love you, you love me, and by the Grace of God we grow old and gray together sharing this truth. God willingly guide us to continual soul connection and growth. Our love strengthening, our trust never wavering. To never part in this life or, ever more, in God's blissful ever after.

DO WHAT'S RIGHT

DO WHAT'S GOOD

DO GOD'S WILL

DO GOD'S WORD

FREEDOM FROM THE
SHAME OF FEAR

Bad things happen to little ones.
They know no better--believe what they're told--
As adults they trust hurt them so.

Ingrained in them shame so deep
For malicious acts done to them in deceit.
The pain and fear buried within
Survival takes over, and they appear to live.

Many years later, lives out of control.
Terror experienced, but no one can know.
All they ever knew was never tell the secrets and lies
That began long ago 'cause you would die.

You no longer remember why or how your life got this way.
You've long before stopped living--don't even remember that day.
Performing IS your life everyday.
Survival to keep up the front.
Busyness, distractions so no one will see all you're not.
Especially you, if you knew the truth.
Somewhere inside your false reality,
You believe without doubt how bad you are indeed.
Not knowing the truth sets you free;
You're in deep denial to protect all the lies--protect me.

They told you you're crazy--they told you you're bad.
That it's all your fault--the shame that you have.
They hurt you, betrayed you, and took your life.
Left you suffering all alone
Believing it's all your fault.

Then you make it go away
So you can live another day.
Later you wonder what's wrong with your life
When nothing is going right.
Denial--protection--set so deep within
To shatter that system seems the end.

As the terror paralyzes your existence,
Shame has lived in you everyday with unspeakable persistence.
You never think to question the shame
And how it so happened to be in your life in the first place.
It just begins to immobilize you
To the point you're a cripple alienated from view.

Then one day--15 years later--
A therapist finally brings hope
And begins to make sense of your life.
Near death for so long,
It's a miracle you're alive.

You begin to grasp the truth.
The shame of the fear all makes sense too.
IT'S NOT YOUR FAULT.

There's no reason to feel shame for your fear it becomes clear.
Anyone in pain and fear for their life
Would be scared and express it just like you
Because long ago people were hurting you.

Then the shame of the fear is dissolved.
You can let your fear flow free,
And you find it does NOT make you crazy.
Long ago expression of fear was repressed
As your feelings never mattered
To those you must trust.

Now that your feelings are free at times
You look around you and feel joy, excitement, and life.
No more performance "trying to be"
To a world of people more important than me.

Now I let my feelings out to speak the truth.
So long ago when feelings turned off, and no one could know.
I'm no longer protecting no one but me,
And I now know the truth sets you free.

Since the shame of fear has moved aside, I can feel again.
I don't care what I feel--just as long as I CAN.
No longer performing how I should be
Instead of living what's inside of me.
I'M COMING ALIVE!
Now I know why others don't wanna die.

When my feelings still feel scary to me,
And I'm afraid to just let me be.
I remember that who else can I be--I'M ME.
After a lifetime of acts to be an image to you,

I'M EXCITED TO LIVE.
GOD LOVES ME.
I'M VALUABLE.
I EXIST.

So everyone who crosses my path
Can take me as I am--I'm way over that.
Needing others love and approval in such a fundamental way.
I'm no longer a dependent child whose needs were betrayed.
I'm a child of God who has taught me the truth:
I'm lovable and valuable WITH or WITHOUT you.

INSANITY

DON'T LET THEM KNOW YOU CARE.
DON'T LET THEM KNOW YOU FEEL.
DON'T LET THEM REACH YOUR HEART,
OR THEY'LL TEAR YOU ALL APART.

THAT'S THE WORST THING YOU CAN DO;
THEN THEY'LL REALLY FUCK WITH YOU.
DON'T BE VULNERABLE TO THEM;
IT WILL KILL YOU IN THE END.

IF YOU DO CARE, ACHE DEEP INSIDE;
DON'T LET THEM KNOW; BURY IT ALIVE.
GOTTA PRETEND EVEN TO YOURSELF--NO FEELINGS HERE--
EVEN ACKNOWLEDGMENT AND THE INTERNAL BATTLE BEGINS.

BAD THINGS HAPPEN INSANITY PATTERN EMERGES:
PAIN, FEAR, TERROR, RAGE, MANIPULATIONS, BETRAYAL, PARANOIA,
MISTRUST, DESTRUCTION, DISTORTIONS.

WANNA MAKE IT GO AWAY,
BUT YOU KNOW IT'S TOO LATE.

TIME TO PICK UP AND START ALL OVER AGAIN;
CLOSING THE DOOR TO ALL EMOTIONS WITHIN.

LOVE TURNED
TO HATE

IT HAS BEEN IMPOSSIBLE TO BE VULNERABLE TO THOSE AROUND ME.
SUCH VULNERABILITY WILL BE USED TO HURT OR BETRAY ME.
I'M NOTICING THIS EVEN IN THE LITTLEST THOUGHTS OF
TAKING THE TINIEST RISKS TOWARD KINDNESS.

ACTUALLY TAKING THOSE RISKS HOW FREEING THAT FEELS;
YET HOW CONFLICTING AS TO DO THAT EQUALS DEATH SOME HOW.
NOW THE FEAR OF DEATH IS LESSENING~
ITS TRUTH WAS IN MY PAST~NOT MY PRESENT~I TELL MYSELF CONSTANTLY.

I CAN ACT DIFFERENTLY TODAY THAN I HAD TO ALL MY LIFE.
MAYBE IT WON'T KILL ME AS I'M ALL GROWN UP NOW.
I AM MAYBE LEARNING TO *NEED* HEALTHILY;
YET I STILL DON'T KNOW HOW TO DO THAT ONE ENTIRELY.

EVEN IF NEAT LITTLE THOUGHTS COME IN MY MIND~
AS LITTLE AS TELLING ROOMMATES THEY CAN WATCH VIDEOS OF MINE.
TO BE NICE, TO BE LOVING, TO GIVE AT ALL~
REQUIRES THE TEENIEST VULNERABILITY WHICH TRIGGERS THE CYCLE.

TO BE VULNERABLE HAS ALWAYS BEEN SO AGAINST ME.
SO PAINFUL BECAUSE THEN I KNOW I CARE. NOW YOU CAN HURT ME~I'M DEAD.
I'M IN FEAR TO GOTO THE PLACE WHERE YOU COULD HURT ME—
BRING UP THAT UNRESOLVED PAIN.

THAT SIDE ALSO LOVES AND NEEDS SO MUCH~
NOT BEARABLE TO STAY THERE FOR LONG.
OR BECOME MEAN~CONFLICTS BEGIN~
WHEN ALL I WANTED TO DO WAS BE NICE TO A FRIEND.

SO FUCKING SAD AND MY EXPERIENCE SINCE SO YOUNG;
YET I AM SEEING MORE NOW, SO THERE IS A SENSE OF FREEDOM.
MAYBE THAT FREEDOM WILL EVENTUALLY BRING SAFETY WITHIN ME
TO RISK MORE~TO LOVE MORE~WITHOUT TRIGGERING ME.

BE ALL THAT I WAS CREATED TO BE
THAT I THINK I REMEMBER BEING SOMEWHERE IN A DREAM.
I DON'T HAVE TO DIE OR WAIT FOR THE ATTACK AFTERWARD.
I'M BEGINNING TO QUESTION THE BELIEF THAT *LOVE HAS TO HURT.*

TO BE VULNERABLE IS TO DIE OR EVEN WORSE.
TO LET SOMEONE KNOW YOU CARE: "YES, I'M ACTUALLY CALLING YOU FIRST."
BECAUSE I CARE~I CARE~JUST BEING HUMAN.
TO ACTUALLY CARE~YET THAT'S ALL IT TAKES~AND THE CYCLE BEGINS.

WHY MUST CARE BE ANOTHER THING TO SHAME OR MORE SO FEAR?
LIKE WHY WOULD CARING EVER EQUAL TERROR?
UNLESS YOU'VE LIVED A LIFETIME LIKE MINE, I SUPPOSE,
WHERE THAT'S EXACTLY WHAT IT MEANT 'TIL I FROZE.

EVERY TIME YOU LOVED OVER AND OVER AGAIN
THAT SENSITIVE CHILD I WAS AND TRULY AM~
UNDER ALL THESE LAYERS OF PAIN, BETRAYAL, MANIPULATION, AND DESTRUCTION~
I WAS SO TERRIBLY HURT UNTIL I FINALLY HAD TO DIE AND GIVE UP HOPE.

I LEARNED A WARPED BELIEF TO OTHERS' PERCEPTIONS
YET NOT DISTORTED BUT *OH SO TRUE* IN MY EXPERIENCE.
IF YOU WANT TO BE LOVED,
YOU BETTER NOT FEEL OR CARE OR LET SOMEONE KNOW.

DO NOT GIVE YOUR HEART, BE SENSITIVE, OR LOVE SOMEONE SO.
YOU BETTER JUST REMAIN ALOOF, UNCARING, COLD, CALLOUS, AND BOLD.
THEN MAYBE AS EMOTIONALLY UNAVAILABLE AS YOU BECOME,
SOMEONE WILL LOVE YOU THEN.

TO HAVE HAD TO LEARN SUCH A TRUTH EXISTED
IN THE ENVIRONMENT AND LIFE I LIVED IN.
I COULDN'T EVEN BE ME: ALIVE, LOVING, FEELING, AND FREE.
AND OTHERS COULD COME TO BELIEVE IN THE HEARTLESS ME.

SHE COULD BECOME SO DEEPLY INGRAINED AND NECESSARY TO MY EXISTENCE
THAT SHE BECAME A PART OF ME WHO I LOVE AND TREASURE DEEPLY.
SHE HAS KEPT ME ALIVE YET THE WORLD DOESN'T SEE HER VALUE~
HER STRENGTH, HER NECESSITY, HER BRILLIANCE~AS A PROTECTOR.

PEOPLE JUST SEE VICKY AS COLD, MEAN, CALLOUS, AND CRUEL.
OH AND, DON'T FORGET, ANGRY AND HATEFUL.
AND YET THE VERY ONES WHO SHOULD POSSIBLY HAVE A CLUE
WALK AROUND EACH DAY MAD AT YOU!

SOMEWHERE INSIDE YOU WISH YOU COULD COME OUT,
BUT YOU'VE LOST YOUR VOICE FOR TOO MANY YEARS NOW.
THE FRUSTRATION AND PAIN BURIED SO DEEP WITHIN~
WISHING YOU COULD MAKE SOMEONE UNDERSTAND AND COMPREHEND.

BUT THERE'S NO POINT IN TRYING TO TALK IT OUT.
YOU'VE LONG SINCE LOST EXPRESSION IN WORDS EXCEPT THROUGH A HOWL.
ONLY A STRANGER COULD POSSIBLY SHOW SOME COMPASSION:
HOW WOULD YOU BEHAVE IF YOU LIVED A LIFE WITHOUT LOVE GIVEN?

LOVE WITHOUT DESPERATE NEED

I am learning to love again.
Feel without utter pain, despair, and doom.
Wishing terror, hate, and shame would go away soon.
I crave to feel longer each day without destruction in the way.

Life without love is death too.
Flat-lined existence and robotic motion becomes you.
Letting the care and vulnerable out.
Realizing what life is all about.

Knowledge that feeling brings life to me.
I may learn love without helpless need.
Loving is caring human emotions expressed.
Normal and vital to all as it breeds happiness.

Others need to know I care, and I need to receive that care.
It is so basic to living I am just now comprehending.
When all my life love taught me something different:
Pain, terror, desperation, hate, shame, and death.

To live again.
To discover love without pain.
Heal Cindy that love child frozen within.
She and I can blend and experience life and love consistent.

Innocent child's love healed inside--
Grieved pain and dependent hunger deprived.
Combined with adult love and mature need
As JWK began teaching me.

THE HOWL

From insanity to death of a soul
And eternal despair and darkness.
To the ceaseless howl years later unleashed--
Raging screams of a lifetime.

Arms swinging, head shaking, and plunging to the ground.
Gut-wrenching screams heightening, heightening,
Heightening . . . totally encompassing throughout.

Shrills escaping their prison within
Harming ears of witnesses trapped inside
These reverberating peripheral walls outside.

Intensity so strong
Reaching, rising, intensifying
Nausea of a forgotten childhood.
Whirling upward and reminding:
Sickness, weakness, helplessness, hopelessness.
Baby wails from hell
Fighting, hitting, beating, screaming. . . .
Punching fists, curling lips
Fetal body mumbling never heard, incoherent words.
Accelerating, piercing, never-ending

Only breaking for moments of breath.
Frantic frenzy, distraught and crazy
Then hurled back into its grasp:
Crying, shrieking, uncontrollable shaking, releasing. . . .

Floods of rage, hate, frustration, sadness, and pain pouring out.
Letting go from the depths within the rage of an innocent child:

I HAVE A VOICE NOW!
YOU DIDN'T KILL ME.
I HAVE A FUCKING VOICE NOW!!

I AM ALIVE.
I MATTER.

I'M NOT CRAZY.
I'M NOT FUCKING CRAZY!!

I MATTER AND I'M NOT PROTECTING NO ONE NO MORE--
NO MORE!
NO MORE SECRETS--NO MORE LIES!

I GIVE IT ALL BACK TO YOU!!!
WHO TOOK MY LIFE.
BUT I DIDN'T DIE.

I SURVIVED.

I MATTER AND I DESERVE LIFE!!!

Denial breakthrough into Sam's freedom and light.
Clouds parting, hope surfacing, heaviness lifting,
Movements swiftening, life mattering,
Despair and depression subsiding,
Mind and brain chemistry changing.

I'm feeling again.
Things are happening in my mind.
Organizing
Feeding me feelings and memories in time.
10 years flew by
And the Lake house and Irvine and
I'm going backward in time.
Layers peeling away and it's all good
I'm healing! It's a miracle! It's amazing!
I'm going back to Cerritos and Glendale and
Wherever else I've Been.
I'M BEING PUT BACK TOGETHER AGAIN.
I can feel it happening inside my mind.
Not understand it--it's beyond my control--yet I trust it.
The brain is powerful I know.

Each moment of doom drifting away
To anticipated moments of *being* each day.
I'm waking in the mornings without complete dread of living.
Voices and meetings conducted inside my head
Like santa's helpers or that book I read
That I connected to--just like it said.

Rose moving aside from the opening door within
Letting all the little ones out to live once again.
Veronica's control lessening so I can have people in my life.

WE'RE FEELING

I'M DESERVING

LIFE'S BEGINNING

IT'S ABOUT TIME

MY LIFE
(Short Story)

FROM FEELING TO DIVIDING

TO FREEZING TO HIDING

TO DARKNESS AND FINALLY BACK TO LIGHT

AND ENTERING THE FROZEN AND DIVIDED SIDES

AND HEALING UNTIL WE ARE ALL ONE

ALIVE AND FLUID HUMAN

WITH VARIOUS EMOTIONS GLIDING TO AND FRO

ONE INDIVIDUAL

ME.

LIVING IS

FEELING

AND

LOVING IS

HEALING

TRANSFORMATION

FROM DESPAIR TO HOPE, FROM DARKNESS TO LIGHT.

FROM BLINDNESS TO VISION, I SEE THINGS CLEARLY--IT'S AMAZING!

FROM ALWAYS GONE TO BECOMING PRESENT.

FROM THE WALKING DEAD TO LIVING.

I NOTICE THINGS, I SEE THINGS, I HEAR THINGS--I'M HERE!

WE'RE TALKING, WE'RE PLAYING, WE'RE LAUGHING--I'M HERE!

FROM DISTORTIONS TO CLARITY, FROM ANXIETY TO PEACE.

NO WONDER PEOPLE WANNA LIVE--I FEEL HAPPY!

FROM NOTHING MATTERS TO GRATITUDE AND HUMAN DESIRE.

IT MATTERS. I CAN HAVE A LIFE. I'M GOOD. I MATTER!

I DESERVE GOOD, I DESERVE HAPPINESS, I DESERVE LIFE, I'M FREE.

THOSE ENDLESS SCREAMS, AND HOWLS FROM HELL.

UNLEASHED MY LIFE--IT'S NOT MY FAULT!

NO MORE SECRETS, NO MORE LIES, I'M COMING ALIVE.

NO MORE INSANITY--I'M NOT CRAZY--BAD PEOPLE HURT ME.

I CAN FEEL THE MIND BUSY AT WORK.

I DON'T UNDERSTAND IT, BUT I TRUST IT, IT'S DOING ME GOOD.

UNLIKE HUMPTY DUMPTY, I'M BEING PUT BACK TOGETHER AGAIN,

'CAUSE IT'S ME MORE AND MORE.

OLD ME'S I REMEMBER FROM WAY BACK WHEN, AND

LIFE I FORGOT THAT I KNEW THEN.

I CAN LIVE. I CAN EAT. I CAN BE SPONTANEOUS.

I CAN SEE A FRIEND--MAYBE WANT TO SEE A FRIEND.

IT CAN MATTER--I MATTER!

I'M SMILING AT PEOPLE. I'M SMILING INSIDE.

TOTAL ANXIETY SLIPPING AWAY

'CAUSE I'M FREE TO BE ME TODAY!

MIRROR IMAGE OF AN
INCEST SURVIVOR

Whatever I believe that I will receive,
I reflect outward, and it shines back at me.

As sure as my belief constitutes love and personal power within,
My self worth flourishes; the sky is the limit!

Just as with God all is possible,
Your reflection is clear so no distortions.

Love understood when His spirit is inside.
No man can break us or make us die.

Devastation of incest remains so destructive.
It takes our self-love and self-worth that was God given.

We reflected innocence, goodness, and purity to
Parental figures we trusted with the truth.

It takes every ounce of our inherent value.
It kills our spirit; we are not worthy now.

We live, eat, and breathe what was taught in a flash:
Powerlessness, hopelessness: A victim--I'm trash.

Everywhere we go and anything we see and all that we do--TAINTED!
Our value is missing. We don't matter. We're not deserving.

Through those eyes we bring forth and cycle
A lifetime repeating what was given as a child.

LOST LIFE

TO YEARN AND DESPERATELY WEEP FOR CONNECTION.

SWALLOWED AND DIGESTED: BETRAYAL, FEAR, AND DESTRUCTION.

YOU WANT TO BE CLOSE; YOU WANT TO FIT IN.

NO CONTROL OF THAT HAPPENING.

YOU ATTEMPT AND RISK AND STRUGGLE EACH TIME.

UNABLE TO HAVE THOSE ESSENTIAL DESIRES AND NEEDS MET OF MINE.

STARTING OVER AGAIN WITH PERSEVERANCE, DETERMINATION, AND STRENGTH.

BELIEVING THIS TIME IT CAN BE DIFFERENT.

I LONG TO EXPERIENCE WHAT OTHERS DO EACH DAY

WITHOUT UTTER TERROR AND DESPAIR IN THE WAY.

That friend; that relationship; that life.
That luncheon; that bullshit talk function.
That meet for coffee and catch up on the scoop.
That kickback and hang and do nothing with you.

That sprawl on the floor and watch t.v. with whomever.
That smile and say "Hi" to a neighbor.
That social event getting to know others.
That continuing to talk to an acquaintance you might see later.

That get together and play games like children.
That spontaneous smile, giggles, and laughter.
That job; that vacation; that dinner engagement.
That hang out and do nothing get together.

That just have fun for no reason.
That superbowl party; that reunion.
That picnic; that birthday; that special occasion.
That wedding; that party; that no biggee function.

JUST DO LIFE

TO BREATHE, RELAX, AND JUST *BE*.

HOW MANY WAYS THE ABUSE HAS AFFECTED ME.

LIVING HAS BEEN IMPOSSIBLE FOR ME.

DEVELOPING A RELATIONSHIP WITH GOD

The more pain you are in
The more you pray.

The more time you spend with God
The more hope you feel.

The more hope you feel
The more your life expands.

The more your life expands
You develop faith.
As the smoother flow of your life unfolds
The more your faith blossoms and grows.

The more your faith blossoms and grows
The more peace you know.

The more peace you know
The more time you spend with God.

The more time you spend with God
The more you know yourself and your value.

The more you know your value
The more you know God's love.

The more you know God's love
The more you love yourself.

The more you love yourself
The more you honor God.

The more you honor God
The more you read the Bible.

The more you read God's word
The love in you grows.

The more the love in you grows
Life becomes a miracle! You become grateful!

The more gratitude you experience
The more you grow to love God.

The more your love for God grows
The more you wish to serve Him.

The more you wish to serve Him
The more you feel His presence, His light, His words.

The more you feel His presence, His light, His words
The more His words make sense.

The more you read God's word
The more you understand.

The more you understand His words
You no longer fear Him as His words are read with loving wisdom.

The more you no longer fear Him
The more you wish to read.

The more you read and understand
The more you love others–God's children–
As others are reflections of yourself as one in Christ.

The more you love others in Christ,
The more you radiate the image of Christ.

The more you radiate the image of Christ–
You live the awesome truth of the oneness of creation–
The bliss of God through Jesus Christ, His Son.

So even when you're upset or wish to do your will,
You find it easier and easier to surrender.
Pray for God's will and a shift in perception–
Miracle letting go and forgiveness.

And amazingly you feel better.
It's out of you—you're free again–it's in God's hands.
Especially when you realize too
Our connection through Christ–everyone is a part of you.

Even when you mess up and have to do it your way,
You know God's word and presence through your relationship
And know that you're okay.
He loves you unconditionally and will never go away.

His divine love for you will bring you to honor Him more.
You'll get back on the right path where you were before.
It's the bliss and peace that keeps you coming back for more.

God so loved us that he wants us–each and every one–
To experience that world of peace and bliss
Through Jesus Christ, His Son.

BREAKING FREE

BREAKING FREE OF THE BINDS OF THIS WORLD

SO OUR SOULS GRASP THE TRUTH, BIG PICTURE, BIGGEST LESSON OF THIS WORLD:

NOTHING OF THIS WORLD MATTERS

IT'S ALL BEEN A JOURNEY OF LIFE UNFOLDING, MUCH SUFFERING AND PAIN

MANY LESSONS BUIL D I N G CHARACTER TOWARD HIGHER LEVELS OF BEING.

OPENING OUR EYES, REACHING OUR SOULS

TEACHING LOVE, COMPASSION, FAITH, HOPE.

PREPARING US, BRINGING US EACH IN PERFECT TIMING

CLOSER TO A TRUE GLIMPSE OF REALITY.

THE BLISS AND JOY, FREE WORLD LAYERS BELOW

PERFECTLY CLEANSED, BROKEN FREE, BACK TO OUR TRUE ESSENCE: PURITY.

SHINING BRIGHT

SPIRITS REFLECTING THE IMAGE OF CHRIST.

SPREADING THE LIGHT, LOVE, ETERNAL WORLD

GOD'S WORLD.

HOW CAN

YOU *BE*

WHEN YOU'RE

TRYING TO BE.

A FOREIGN WORLD
(LOVE)

ONE DAY REALITY HIT ME, A TRUTH I NEVER KNEW.
HIS ACTIONS MEANT HE LOVED ME; I NEVER REALLY KNEW.
THEN THE PAIN AND SECOND ACTUALITY SUDDENLY CAME MY WAY:
NO ONE EVER LOVED ME IN A PROPER WAY.
THAT'S HOW COME I NEVER KNEW, NEVER TRUSTED, NEVER BELIEVED.
HOW DO I RECOGNIZE IN SOMEONE ELSE SOMETHING I NEVER RECEIVED.

HOW OFTEN NOW AS I RE-PLAY THE MANY TIMES WE SPENT,
I KNOW MY EYES DIDN'T SEE, AT THE TIME, WHAT HIS BEHAVIOR MEANT.
I WAITED, AND I WONDERED JUST WHAT WAS UP HIS SLEEVE.
I NEVER KNEW ANYTHING BUT PAIN, BETRAYAL, AND DECEIT.
EVEN WHEN I BEGAN TO TRUST HIM AND LET HIM REACH MY HEART,
THE TERROR THAT CAME OUT TORE ME ALL APART.
THEN IT JUST REMINDED ME OF HOW IT HAS TO BE:
YOU LOVE ME, AND MAYBE I RECEIVE.
BUT NEVER LET MY LOVE FOR YOU BE EVER SEEN--ESPECIALLY TO ME.

IT HURTS TO WANT TO LOVE MORE THAN YOU COULD EVER KNOW.
BUT TO DO THAT FEELS LIKE DEATH TO ME--IT'S IMPOSSIBLE.
YOU SHOW ME MORE TRUST THAN I EVER KNEW.
I BEGIN TO LEARN LOVE DOESN'T HAVE TO EQUAL PAIN THROUGH YOU.
I BEGIN TO LOVE YOU, THE CLOSER WE BECAME.
I NEVER QUITE LET YOU KNOW SO WE COULD STAY SAFE.
EVEN DENIED TO ME MY LOVE FOR YOU,
SO OUR RELATIONSHIP WOULDN'T END, AND I COULD BE WITH YOU.

SOME OF ME BEGINS TO ACT IN WAYS YOU DO NOT LIKE.
YOU SAID YOU WERE STRONG AND COULD STAY STILL;
i KNEW IT WAS IMPORTANT AND BELIEVED YOU WERE GOD'S WILL.
YET EVEN THE SLIGHTEST THING YOU DO, MAKES ME GO AWAY.
LOVING TAUGHT ME SO LONG AGO, i WILL ONLY BE BETRAYED.
AT THE POINT YOU LOVE SOMEONE, THEY'LL SURELY GO AWAY,
AND EVERY OUNCE OF LOVE BRINGS ME CLOSER TO THAT DAY.

HOW DO YOU TEACH YOURSELF A COMPLETELY DIFFERENT TRUTH
WHEN THE CLOSER TO LOVE YOU GET THE INSANITY BEGINS TO UNFOLD,
AND THE LITTLE ONES ARE THE ONLY ONES IN CONTROL?
NO ONE UNDERSTANDS ME, AND i CAN'T QUITE MAKE IT STOP.
ALL i EVER WANTED WAS TO BE LOVED, AND IT'S ALL i NEVER GOT.
AFTER A WHILE WHEN YOU'RE TIRED OF IT ALWAYS GOING AWAY,
YOU WANNA STOP LOVING ALTOGETHER FOR SANITY'S SAKE.
GIVE UP SOONER BEFORE THE PATTERNS BEGIN AGAIN.
NO ESCAPE FROM ALL YOU'VE EVER KNOWN AND ALL YOU'VE EVER BEEN.

SO YOU WATCH YOUR LIFE UNFOLD PRAYING AND HOPING FOR THE DAY
YOU MAY LOVE SOMEONE BACK, AND THEY'LL NEVER GO AWAY
OR HURT YOU SO YOU CAN STAY.
LATER YOU REALIZE THAT UNTIL THE LITTLE ONES ARE HEALED--
IT'S AN IMPOSSIBILITY AS YOU WILL BE HURT--THEN THE CYCLE BEGINS.
OH, HOW MANY TIMES THE HOPE *THIS* TIME i CAN TRULY LOVE.
i'M ALRIGHT NOW--i CAN DO IT--i KNOW IT CAN BE DIFFERENT NOW
ONLY TO HAVE THE INSANITY BEGIN ALL OVER AGAIN.
THEN YOU COMPREHEND FOR A WHILE--STAY THE HELL AWAY FROM MEN!
UNTIL THE DESIRE FOR LOVE BECOMES TOO STRONG AGAIN.

i BEGAN TO ACTUALLY BELIEVE FOR A TIME THAT MY DREAMS JUST MIGHT COME TRUE.
YET IN THE END, HE BECAME THE ENEMY, AND i BELIEVE HAS REPRESSION TOO.

ONCE THE PING PONG BALL BEGINS TO BOUNCE
i KNOW THIS IS THE TIME WE MUST HURRY AND GET OUT.
HOW MUCH DO YOU WANNA LOVE AND HURT THIS TIME WE SAY?
BEFORE SANITY BEGINS AGAIN AND THE LITTLE ONES
BECOME TERRIFIED, WE CONTROL, OR HE GOES AWAY.
HE SAYS "DON'T YOU FIGHT FOR WHAT YOU WANT?!"
HE TRIES TO TELL ME "WE CAN BE" IF THAT IS WHAT WE WANT.
THEN i REALIZE HE DOESN'T HAVE A CLUE
EVEN KNOWING ALL ABOUT ME HE HAS NOT DIGESTED THE TRUTH.
WHAT IT IS LIKE INSIDE OF ME--WHAT IS GOING ON--i HAVE NO PROOF.
EXCEPT THAT IT CONTROLS MY LIFE AND IF IT COULD WILL DESTROY YOU.
BECAUSE i REALLY LOVE YOU, i'D RATHER END RIGHT NOW,
SO YOU WILL REMEMBER ME WITH RESPECT AND LOVE IN YOUR HEART.
INSTEAD OF LOOKING BACK ON MEMORIES OF ME
AS A NICE GIRL TURNED PSYCHO YOU DATED TEMPORARILY.

IF i COULD SHRIEK THE LOUDEST SHRILL SO EVERYONE COULD HEAR,
IF IN THOSE SCREAMS YOU COULD SEE MY HEART AND HOW i REALLY FEEL,
THEN, AT LEAST, i WOULD FEEL GOOD TO KNOW YOU UNDERSTOOD
HOW VERY MUCH i LOVE YOU AND WANTED THIS TO WORK.
HOW HOPELESS AND FRUSTRATING MY EXISTENCE HAS BEEN.
IT'S NOT ABOUT NOT WANTING LOVE--IT'S ABOUT REPETITIVE REALITIES WITHIN.
i CANNOT DENY NO MORE BECAUSE WHETHER OR NOT i PRETEND,
THE PATTERNS WILL STILL EMERGE FROM WITHIN.
THE LONGER WE'RE TOGETHER, THE WORSE IT WILL BECOME.

DON'T YOU SEE I'VE GIVEN YOU MY HEART; THE BATTLE WITHIN BEGINS.
AREN'T WE LUCKY!? YOU'LL LOSE, WE LOSE--THEY ALWAYS WIN.

YOU WERE BETTER OFF LOVING ME WITHOUT MY LOVING YOU BACK
OR MY LOVING SILENTLY, FROM WAY IN THE BACK, WHERE YOU NEVER KNEW.
THE MOMENT I ACKNOWLEDGE IT TO MYSELF--THAT INSTANT I WANT TO KILL YOU.
THEN, THE ROLLER COASTER RIDE STARTS UP.
AREN'T YOU LUCKY!? I'VE GIVEN YOU MY HEART!

AS MUCH AS I WANT TO LOVE YOU, EVEN MORE NOW THAN BEFORE,
THIS IS WHERE I WATCH HOW I DESTROY YOU AND LET YOU GO.
THEN AT SOME POINT DOWN THE LINE, I COME BACK AND MISS YOU SO.
BUT REALIZE ONCE AGAIN HOW IT IS, AND I JUST GET TO ACHE AND MOURN.
I LOVE YOU STILL AND HAD JUST ADMITTED THAT TO MYSELF,
WHEN I BOUGHT THOSE CARDS, BEFORE THE PING PONG BALL BEGAN TO BOUNCE.
THAT'S WHEN I KNEW I WANTED TO SPEND MY LIFE WITH YOU--WITHOUT A DOUBT.

THE CONFUSING THING I'M BEGINNING TO KNOW AS I HEAL IN RECOVERY
IS THAT WHAT I SEE AND FEEL--MY TRUTH--IS NOT REALITY.
I WALK ALONG AND VIEW MY PRESENT WORLD THROUGH EYES OF A FORGOTTEN TIME.
I DON'T EVEN KNOW I'M IN--IT COMPLETELY BLOWS MY MIND!
HOW DO YOU EVER SEE A WORLD--THIS WORLD--THROUGH EYES CLEARLY TODAY
WHEN YOUR WORLD AND YOUR VISION KEEPS CHANGING WITHIN MOMENTS OF EVERYDAY
ACCORDING TO WHOSE SIDES' EMOTIONS ARE TRIGGERED OUT
BASED ON SOMETHING OF THIS WORLD TRIGGERING THEIR WORLD THAT YOU FORGOT?!

NOW YOU FACE YOU MAY NOT SEE CLEARLY MOST THE TIME.
YOU NOTICE HOW MUCH YOU DON'T HEAR AND SEE MORE TIMES THAN YOU WOULD LIKE.

AS YOU BECOME TRIGGERED, OR ARE WALKING THROUGH YOUR LIFE,
YOU WONDER NEXT, HOW DO I KNOW: IS THIS TRUTH OR A LIE?
I'M NOT SURE MOST THE TIME WHAT IS REAL OR MAKE BELIEVE
FROM A PAST I'M STILL RECOVERING TO GAIN SOME SANITY.
WHO DO I TRUST TO ASK FOR TRUTH TO GAIN CLARITY--
ESPECIALLY WHEN DEEP INSIDE EVERYONE'S THE ENEMY?

THE HAUNTING TRUTH: NO ONE EVER LOVED ME AS I SO DESERVED
TO THE POINT 30 YEARS LATER HIS LOVE SENT ME
TO A TIME AND PLACE WHEN OTHERS DID ME WRONG.
THAT FOR ME BECAME WHAT LOVE EQUATED AND WHERE IT WILL LEAD ME TO:
A NITEMARE LONG DENIED SOMEWHERE IN MY PAST--THE TRUTH.
IF NO ONE EVER LOVED ME HEALTHILY--
AND I GREW UP BLOCKED FROM EMOTIONS FROZEN IN TIME,
NEVER EXPERIENCING LOVE OR GIVING LOVE OF MINE--
NO WONDER ALL THOSE MANY YEARS I FEARED I'M A SOCIOPATH
AS HOW COULD SOMEONE NEVER LOVED, EVER LOVE SOMEONE ELSE BACK?

YOU BECOME CONSCIOUS ENOUGH TO HEAR WHAT OTHERS SAY.
YOU COMPREHEND THEIR FACIAL EXPRESSIONS AND BODY LANGUAGE.
ASK QUESTIONS TO LEARN ANOTHER WAY--
WHERE MAYBE YOU COULD STAY PRESENT IN TODAY.
THEN, IN FLASHES YOU RE-PLAY MANY OTHER DAYS
YOU DIDN'T EVEN KNOW YOU DIDN'T KNOW AND WALKED AWAY.

IT HAD TO BE A MIND FUCK--A GAME AT MY EXPENSE.
HOW COULD HE REALLY LOVE ME? IT'S ALL PRETEND.
EVEN IF HE LOVED ME WHAT DO I COMPARE THAT TO

TO RECOGNIZE LOVE STARING ME IN THE FACE--
A FOREIGN WORLD I NEVER KNEW.

BY THE GRACE OF GOD IN RECOVERY,
A LOVING ADULT WAS CREATED OR DEVELOPED INSIDE OF ME.
SHE BEGAN TO TEACH ME HOW TO LOVE HEALTHILY WITHOUT THE NEED.
BUT THROUGH TAMMY AND A LIFETIME, WITHOUT A DOUBT I KNOW,
UNTIL MY SIDES ARE HEALED LASTING LOVE'S IMPOSSIBLE.

I PUT MEN ON A HIDDEN SHELF AS THE LITTLE ONES HEAL INSIDE.
I GOTO THE LONELY PLACE I'VE KNOWN ALL MY LIFE.
THE DIFFERENCE IS I'M HEALING THIS TIME AROUND.
I'LL ACCESS MY SIDES, SPECIFICALLY THE NEED,
IN THE SAFE, TRUSTING ENVIRONMENT OF THERAPY.

WHEN ALL I'VE EVER WANTED
AND DIDN'T RECEIVE AS A CHILD NEEDS--
SOMEDAY I CAN'T WAIT TO FIND DIFFERENTLY ONCE I'VE GRIEVED:
A TRULY HEALTHY ADULT LOVE,
A CHRISTIAN MAN TO SHARE HIS LIFE WITH ME.

FLUID EMOTIONS

A glimpse into another world where feelings flow to and fro. Fluid like a forgotten day when emotions were free to come out and play. A time of freedom; life takes its course. It's all okay; life just goes that way.

Life will once again be free feeling and being all of me. Various smooth transitions--neither frozen nor compartmentalized. No longer a different world--always-changing vision--a different life depending on whose eyes are out to see at times. I look so forward to the day, gliding from one emotion to the next, expressing, flowing, ever-changing. So eloquently swirling amid the changing colors--beauty and peace--inconsistency so complete.

When such a glimpse comes my way, I hold to the memory I'm healing. And as I switch from side to side, I grasp I'm not really living another life. As each day I heal, they are ALL me and though so different their perceptions, reality, energy, desires, experiences, and behavior may seem, I'm becoming free--every facet of me. And soon not worlds apart, going to the OTHER side, but instead reaching and accessing ME as ONE life. Fluttering feelings anew each day, excitement, enjoyment, peace, contentment. Never wandering a moment ahead. Trusting the outcome each day will bring--just BEING--so freeing--a life should be.

With fluid emotions so many lives behind you, tracks more like traces by now dust unseen. Trapped inside--moments of expression--when terror and pain have come your way and living--not dying--seems far away. You forget you remembered another way; a far off day when you were allowed to play. And then a moment reminds you of a life you thought you dreamed. And it all makes sense: But, of course, this is the way it's supposed to be! A time when life--the ebb and flow--was so normal and once was known.

Before they took it all away and you forgot you knew another way. Except now, more and more as you see light, you hope the dream may be right. There will be a day not far away when it won't be a flicker--a flash untrue--of a stolen life I'll see. Instead I'll be living--it'll be me. My feelings--my sides--all as one. We'll coast from day to day, hour to hour, moment to moment, feeling and breathing and hearing and seeing, in and out and to and from all spontaneous feelings as We become One.

So wherever I go on a given day, whether I'm playful or fearful or kind or mean; ashamed or alive or fear you may look at me; loving or hurting, grown-up or small; likable or tolerable or the despairing one. No matter if I'm fun or gone or free, I'm learning just to be me. No longer must we perform to gain approval or safety to fulfill your desires--hiding in the shadows--or spend our life perfecting images we called life. After years of hiding, we are alive. Learning to surface more and more, fragile and scared in bodies we'd left behind, and now healing and breathing and experiencing life.

So we live everyday life--not for anyone no more--as that life made us die. And as we walk through our memories, insecurities, shames, pain, and fear, we accept and love and embrace our tears. And all we encounter and who surround us out there that may trigger and bring us fear, who could stifle our growth through the years, we no longer need to get from them--the acceptance, safety, approval, and love lost so long ago--what God and therapy is bringing within. Out of the tunnel: Seeing and hearing and knowing more clearly each day--it's getting easier to just be me--fluid emotions more consistent and free.

THERE WAS A TIME WHEN I LIKED TO

LIVE AND LAUGH AND PLAY

AND THEN ONE DAY

IT WENT AWAY.

D O O M

Each day, each moment, each step a dread
I never wanted to get out of bed.
The mornings were a time to avoid
Even if I woke, I'd close my eyes.
Showering became a necessity
As four to five days would pass by,
And the task of bathing seemed too hard to try.
Food was just shoveled into my mouth.
Got to eat so I don't wither away; run and follow rituals
Just to get through another day.

I really could care less how I look
At home, meetings, therapy, errands, running, or body work.
Wear the same old thing--my favorite baggy sweatshirt.
Didn't have to worry about laundry, and I never cooked.
Hair thrown up high in a pony tail, so no one knew
How long since I brushed my hair or shampooed.
Even going down the stairs to juice took all my strength.
I felt so weak--everything bothered me.
Darkness surrounded me--I felt drained.
I would hear neighbors or roommates talk or laugh,
And it was like another world far away where I didn't exist.

I knew that running was my strength
Yet I would cry throughout stretching
Or trance out so I could complete.
On the worst and heaviest days
I would tell myself we're not going today.
But I knew how bad it already is,
If I don't run, I won't make it--that's for sure.
Just going to do this neck stretch and then goto bed.
Then as my body was doing situps
I'd still believe, I'm going to stop--goto sleep.
Sometimes even as I drove to the beach
I'd be convincing myself--turn around--it's got you beat.
Yet there we'd be once again at the beach
Running seven miles keeping our strength.

To most people time there just isn't enough of
My thought about time was something to get out of.
Each moment tick ticking away
Doom was always near throughout my day.
I constantly had to reassure myself
The way I feel is not real today.
These feelings are from long ago
Because there's nothing in my given day
That should make me feel this way.
The thought that this may be permanent was too much to bear
So got to have hope from my despair.
Each moment seemed to drag on by,
And I would just wanna die.

Even when time passed me by,
My future seemed so bleak,
The walls caving in on me.
How do you explain?
Make sense of what it's like?
Every waking moment in a world where time is treasured.
Yet for me each waking hour feels like pressure.
Like I wonder what now--what's going to happen next?
A big empty void and aching inside.
Where I can't wait for the day to end and I survived
Only to realize tomorrow will repeat
What today had in store for me.
I can't bare to walk through these feelings--
This void--this dark black hole.
Even God must be ashamed and hate me
As all hope is bleeding away from me.
My existence so full of pain and dread
And where I should be grateful
I wish I were dead.

No one understands as I wonder which is worse:
Endless terror and panic attacks?
Or darkness--complete emptiness--blackhole abyss?
Where you try to pretend--distract and waste time
So you can make it--get through another night.
Program taught me feelings can't kill you.
But then each moment trudges by.
You feel you're bouncing out of your skin
With anxiety and depression living within.

Tammy says only my actions can hurt me
So I make a contract with her for my life and keep a copy.

If living each day has to feel like this,
What's the point? What's my purpose?
The world seems far away.
You wonder what would happen if you just didn't move.
Would somebody notice? How long after?
Would it matter? What would happen to you?
All the scenarios of your last breath
And God and a brother
Whom you don't know how to say good-bye to yet.
You wonder what will be the final straw?
Where death is worth the risk to your life
To the point you're gone?
Then you understand all about hell
As you're living it on earth.
The truth hits you: If hell is living inside you,
Even if you die, your soul is not at rest.
It will be hell for your spirit,
Which has been your only life.

Thinking the only way through is taking pills to tranquilize.
Yet somehow you're too bright--You already put addictions aside.
You've struggled a lifetime to heal--
That's why you're still here--you're a survivor still.
Even though you can't feel without panic inside;
The pills only make you dead which is how you feel all the time.

Don't give up now with Tammy on your side;
You're healing; you're getting better;
It just doesn't feel good right now.
Don't let who hurt you win after all this time,
And all you've been through you've already survived.

Some memories and dreams and another anger letter to dad.
Somehow you access and act out your rage and how!
You scream, cry, holler, and shake
And beat and wail your fury from hell.
Somehow you open prison's gate from within.
The possibility your life may actually begin.
As life begins to come out of you,
It's a miracle what begins to happen.
You begin to notice and remember the basics you now can do.
You recognize this is living--
That's what has been missing in you.

I can read, I can play, I can talk to someone.
I can goto the mall, or I can get my hair done.
I can buy me a candy bar just because I want one.
I can stop in the middle of my day just for an icecream sundae.
I can lay on my bed and do absolutely nothing.
Just look out the window and reflect--I can be.

You sometimes get a glimpse of time from the past
When life mattered within but you're not quite sure when.
Is it real or pretend those long ago years taken from you?
Only darkness to face so you forgot what you knew.

'Cause now as new life and light comes your way,
You become grateful for this very day.
You hear words from within chanting to you:

"There was a time when I liked to

live and laugh and play

And then one day it went away."

Then you realize that day is coming back again,
And no one will ever take your life from you--that was a sin.
You made it through the deep black hole dug for you.
You escaped and are healing and believe you'll get through.

SO MANY PEOPLE

SO MANY LIVES

I'VE BEEN BROKEN

TOO MANY TIMES

THE PARADOX
(WALKING THROUGH DARKNESS BRINGS LIGHT)

ONLY BY LOOKING AT AND INTO THE DARKEST REALMS OF YOU—
WHO YOU THINK YOU ARE OR FORGOT THAT YOU KNEW—
WILL THAT LIGHT SHED ON THE DARK AS YOU CONTINUE TO VIEW,
FADE THE DARKNESS SO THAT IT SLIPS AWAY FROM YOU.

THEN YOU CAN SEE THE TRUTH OF THE BEAUTY OF YOU
UNDERNEATH THE LAYERS OF DARK THAT BECAME YOU.
THE TRUTH OF YOUR EXISTENCE
FAR FROM WHAT YOU REMEMBERED OR EVER KNEW.

IF EVERYONE ONLY KNEW HOW PEACEFUL AND FREEING LIFE COULD BE
TO WANDER A TIME IN THE DARKNESS
PEELING AWAY LAYERS AND COMING OUT CLEAN.
INSTEAD OF THE SLOW ROT IN HELL—CLUELESS
FROM MISERY WITHIN YOU FORGOT—
YET ACTING OUT IN YOU SO WELL LIVING WHEREVER YOU ARE.

BUT IT NEVER GOES AWAY;
IT LIVES INSIDE YOU EVERYDAY.
WHETHER OR NOT YOU CHOOSE TO LOOK;
IT LIVES RIGHT OUT OF YOU LIKE IT OR NOT.
AND YOUR FEAR TO KNOW ITS TRUTH,
IS, IN FACT, KILLING YOU.

YOUR LIFE IS SPENT CREATING AN IMAGE OF YOU
SO OTHERS WON'T SEE WHAT YOU FEAR IS THE TRUTH.
INSTEAD OF JUST LIVING INSIDE WHO YOU TRULY ARE
IF YOU FACED THE DARK AND THEN BECOME WHO YOU FORGOT.
THE ONLY OTHER OPTION IS TO PRETEND
OUT OF FEAR OF WHO YOU THINK YOU'LL FIND WITHIN.

THE PROCESS OF "TRYING TO BE"
INSTEAD OF JUST *BEING* EASILY
MAKES ALL THE DIFFERENCE IN THE WORLD
AS TO YOU LIVING OR JUST GETTING BY
AS MUCH EFFORT IS WASTED WHEN YOUR GOAL IS TO HIDE.

UNTIL YOU TAKE THE JOURNEY AND ARE SAVED INSIDE OUT.
THEN YOU'LL FIND YOUR TRUE LOVE AND VALUE
AND REALIZE WHAT LIFE IS ALL ABOUT.

FROM FLAT-LINED
TO FEELING

VERONICA IS LETTING GO OF ALL OUR FEELINGS AND CONTROL.
ROSE IS MOVING TO THE SIDE--THE DOOR IS OPENING--*WE'RE ALIVE.*

ALL THE LITTLE ONES ARE THERE.
RUNNING FREE--THEY JUST DON'T CARE.

LOOK AT ME!--I'M HERE!
ONCE AGAIN ALIVE IN ME.

IT'S A BLESSING TO BE SET FREE
FROM PRISON'S WALLS INSIDE OF ME.

ALL THESE YEARS CAPTURED WITHIN
'TILL VERONICA GAINED CLARITY.
SHE REALIZED "FINE" WAS JUST AN ACT.
THE ONLY WAY TO BE REAL AND HEAL
IS TO FEEL US AND CONNECT.

ONCE THOSE SCREAMS EMERGED, WE MATTERING RETURNED.
THERE WAS HOPE FROM NOW ON.
HATRED OUT THERE, NO LONGER TRAPPED INSIDE, AND WE DON'T WANNA DIE.
WE ARE COMPLETELY BLOWN AWAY AS WE GO ABOUT OUR DAY.

NOW WE TRY WITH ALL OUR MIGHT
TO DESIRE EACH DAY—CONNECTION—LIFE.
TO GOTO THE PLACE MORE AND MORE
WHERE IT MATTERS: *PEOPLE—FEELINGS—LOVE.*

WHERE YOU GO FOR COFFEE WITH A FRIEND
BECAUSE YOU CARE—THERE'S LIFE WITHIN.
AND THEN IT MAKES IT ALL WORTH WHILE
AS WHEREVER YOU GO—YOU SMILE.

I'M HERE.

YOU DON'T HAVE TO ISOLATE
BECAUSE BEING WITH OTHERS IS SUCH A DRAIN
TO PRETEND YOU FEEL WHEN YOU'RE DEAD INSIDE.
OR MAKE OTHERS THINK YOU'RE JUST GREAT
WHEN DEEP INSIDE YOU'RE FILLED WITH HATE.
OR EVEN WORSE WHEN YOU WANNA DIE
AND MUST FACE THE WORLD WHEN YOU WANNA HIDE.

AND AS YOU GOTO WHERE YOU CARE AND FEEL,
IT MAKES ALL THE DIFFERENCE IN THE WORLD.
YET YOU STILL PUSH OTHERS AWAY
AS TRIGGERS EVERYDAY.
WHEN YOU DON'T, THEY GO AWAY.
YOUR SKILLS ARE NOT ADULT, OR YOU TALK TOO MUCH THEY SAY.
OR YOUR NEED IS PRESENT, AND THEY STRAY.

OR THEY CAN TELL YOU DON'T FEEL THAT DAY,
OR VICKY'S HATE IS ON DISPLAY.
AND YOU KNOW HOW MANY PEOPLE HAVE GONE AWAY—
SHE SEES ENEMIES EVERYDAY.
EVEN THOUGH SHE'S NOT ALL OF YOU—
THEY SEE YOUR BODY AND THINK IT'S YOU—LIKE YOU USE TO.

OR EVERYTIME YOU START TO FEEL,
THE PAIN IS REACHED YOU HAVE NOT HEALED.
THEN YOU HURT AND WANNA CRY
OR STOP FEELING AND WANNA DIE.

WHEN THE MAN YOU LOVE WAS THERE,
YOU'RE TOO AFRAID HE'LL GO AWAY,
YOU LEAVE HIM BEFORE HE LEAVES YOU SOME DAY.

THEN YOU GOTO SEE A NEW FRIEND,
AND YOU FEEL UNSAFE WITHIN.
YOU'RE STUCK SOMEWHERE BETWEEN FEELING SIDES—
FEELING OR NOT CARING—WHICH ONE WILL SUFFICE?
CANNOT TALK—UNCOMFORTABLE ANXIETY RULES—
AS THEY REACT TO YOUR SOCIAL SKILLS.
AND YOU DON'T KNOW WHAT TO DO
BUT TO GET OUT OF THERE BEFORE YOU'RE RUDE.
WHEN YOU'RE NOT QUITE SURE WHAT YOU DO,
BUT TIME AND TIME AGAIN PROVES—IT'S YOU.

AND ALL THESE FEELINGS FROM LONG AGO;
YOU TRY TO HEAL OR TRY NOT TO SHOW.
AND WHEN YOU DO, THE CYCLE BEGINS.
IT ANGERS YOU—YOU CAN NOT WIN!

SO WHY CAN'T YOU JUST BE BETTER, YOU WISH,
AS HEALING GOES SO SLOW.
YOU'RE TIRED
AND YOU WANNA FEEL, AND YOU CANNOT FEEL.
OR SOME SIDES OF YOU EMBARRASS YOU,
AND THERE'S SO MUCH YOU DON'T KNOW.

SO TRY AND ACCEPT EACH DAY
THE LIMITS ON LOVING WE CAN DISPLAY.
AND NOT HATE MYSELF TODAY
WHEN I'M UNABLE TO RESPOND OR FEEL
AND GO INSIDE AS WE HEAL.
IT'S ALL PART OF MY JOURNEY BACK TO LIFE
AS A WHOLE HUMAN BEING
WITH MANY VARIATIONS IN BETWEEN.

CLOUDY
VISION

Our vision becomes clear;
   It's a beautiful sight.
Like a beautiful, cloudless day
   Amid the moments of utter death-like rage.
Where we see so clearly that we fear
   Do we have the capacity to kill? IS THAT CAPACITY IN HERE?
When we wanna kill them for all we lost.
   For all they took--for all they got.
The more we heal, the more rage we feel.
   As we see and know our loss as the blinders continue to part.
We begin to see and know what those damages are
   And what that looks like so far.
We heal and see the difference unbeknown to once ignorant eyes.
   Just trying to survive and not knowing why.
Comprehension to what's been done inside
   Utter destruction will we come out of this alive?
The rage and pain has had a deathgrip on us
   For more years than most survive it.
And fear that's been our only life
   Glimpses now and again of a different kinda life.
We know this is what sanity, healing love, and true life feels like.
   When clouds part from our eyes, and we dream a clear vision of life.

BEING

BEING IS LIVING EACH MOMENT OF EACH DAY

EXACTLY AS I FEEL TODAY.

LIVING MY FEELINGS INSIDE OF ME

ACCORDING TO HOW I FEEL AND SOOOO . . .

THE EXTERIORS OF LIFE ARE JUST BONUSES, YOU KNOW.

AS LIFE IN ME CONTINUES TO GROW,

BEING IS EASY, AND LIFE FLOWS.

NOBODY, NO MONEY, NO "THINGS" I USED TO NEED

TO REPAIR THE BROKENNESS INSIDE OF ME

THAT NOW IS HEALING AND BECOMING FREE.

ROLE OF
A LIFETIME

When the feelings stop, the performing begins.
Your life is halted; shame sets in.
You must not tell; you must behave normally.
How do you know how to be when you feel nothing internally?
What do you base appropriate on when your feelings are all gone?

The burden--the shame--the game.
Life's a game of pretend; no one must know what lay deep within.
Smile and look alright to the world.
Copy others and how they behave, so you blend in and seem okay.
Mimic emotions and laughter and tears
Don't let anyone know, see the emptiness and hollow in here.
Just as long as everyone thinks you're alright.
That's all that's been important in your life.
Besides what would you do if they knew?
Then, you would be bad and shameful too.
Somewhere from deep within you wish you could just start over again.
Everything would be okay, and you wouldn't have to pretend another day.
But with every passing day,
You don't remember what it was like before that day.

Some days you wonder what is wrong with you
When others feel but how 'bout you?
When the smile is plastic, and the laughter is frozen,
Life in you is gone--a performance.
When you wonder how you'll pass the test
Wherever you go when you feel like an act.

Like I just wanna run and laugh and play
But no feelings to display--they have all been taken away.

Deep within hoping I look alright
As I become each role to fool the world--and make myself think I'm real!
As I get older I wonder too, What the hell is wrong with you?
I've done so well, I've covered my tracks, am I a fucking sociopath?
Whenever the hatred gets too strong, I wonder why God has kept me here so long.
I just wanna do myself in. I think of my precious bro--that is not a lie I know.
I love him deeply so somewhere inside there is love in me alive.

Then I meet Dan who reaches my heart.
No one else could come near, that was made sure of through the years.
And for moments I truly feel; then I want to kill.
I want to pay back for all I lost--and all I'm not.
Not quite understanding what I do or why I would ever want to hurt you.
Then, the panic attacks begin; I'm reliving the terror of childhood over again.
I was relieved when they went away, but they're back 10 years later and I'm awake.
I have no idea what the hell is going on with me--
There is something terribly wrong with me.
Between the terror, depression, moods, and tears I wish to hide,
My life's completely out of control--and that's no lie.

I find a savior that helps for a while
To calm the symptoms and the pain that never really go away.
Even when I try to love you; it's insanity; I'm bouncing; sometimes I scare you.
But some how you see through me. You find my heart; you hold the key.
My moods keep changing, my behavior too,
And it appears to worsen because I love you.

I goto nine therapists for the next 13 years
To make me the way I use to be before the symptoms began killing me.
But no one knows what is wrong with me--
Medications, diagnoses--that don't set me free.
You stick right by me through thick and thin
And tell me to be me wherever I am.
Somewhere deep within we know, but no consciousness to put words to it all.
So, at times, we wonder *Uh Oh, We're not doing our jobs well enough.*
He'll catch on to our act and find out we are a sociopath.
But time passes and no matter what, he loves us more and tells us that.

WHEN WE ARE MEAN AND HURTFUL TOO, HE THINKS WE'RE CUTE AND LOVES US TOO.
And he never goes away--calls us his **ROUGH TOUGH** Cream Puff
AND WE WANNA STAY--HE THINKS WE'RE OKAY.
Even when he can't reach me, he knows I'm here--way in the back--
And I love him too, and he knows that.

Then addiction places me in a cage
No longer my savior--cell's getting smaller each day.
By this time--six years later--I'm agoraphobic.
Quit drinking, but can't even goto the mailbox.
Program teaches me how to live; accept my sides and take small risks.

By this time I've lost more jobs than I recall
Attitude problems, personality conflicts, symptoms and all.
All my sides protecting me from an unsafe world in our past
As they live inside of me, unhealed, projecting out *their* world.
People say leave your past in the past if they only had a clue.
We've tried that route; it's useless too when your past is living inside of you.

Others have no idea how it hurts so bad to wanna love you.
But if we do, it destroys us, and we destroy you.
When it only takes two months at the same job,
And the minimal intimacy that entails, yet my sides are terrified--
Blowing the job all to hell.
Making sure to keep others away, so we can function through the day.
Making enemies of the ones we are getting to know, so they'll leave us alone.
Yet deep inside somewhere we watch--
Wishing we could take it all back and keep our friendships in tact.

But after years of this go on, we give up.
Accept that we must be pretty mean and bad to push others away like that.
And spend our lives alone usually
So the ones inside remain calm, and we can seemingly go on.

Seven years of sobriety brought me tools
Accept my sides without hate so I could love me, *Wouldn't that be great?*
I had come to know my *moods*, how I act, and what I do
And love myself no matter who.
Our marriage--the rollercoaster ride we're on
Until it's over--after 10 years we're gone.
Two lives going separate ways
But I'll never regret the unconditional love and value he brought my way.

People tell you how strong you are; we're just trying to hold on.
Desperation makes you do whatever is necessary to heal you.
Determination, perseverance, and strength.
Running--God to get us through each day.
Many gifts from God come our way
When we wonder if we'll make it another day.

In two years time without our man, things start to get out of hand.
We begin to re-build our life but are triggered left and right.
After years unhealed repression and pain,
Survival took over again--we stayed the same.
After we left, unknown sides began to come out.
We began wondering *Who is that?*
We started over and thought we'd die,
But we get to get better, and it's about time.

After thirteen years of the battle within
Our life is changed--we are saved--it's not too late.
God brings us a therapist who
We tell from the very start--about how we get and how we are.
There is a side of us who makes others go away.
I never told this to anyone before but I'm afraid.
I can't live like this another day.
She promised us no matter who comes out she'd never go away.
We'd have to fire her or she'd stay.

Everytime we lose another job--
We pick ourselves up and strive to carry on.
I tell her *I lost one again--can't do it no more.*
I have no funds to pay for therapy--survival all over again.
She said don't worry about that; job or no job, we're welcome back.
As we stop, survival steps aside,
And all the broken, wounded ones eventually come out and cry.

Although my sides are real; Tammy says all a part of me.
Never knowing who I'll be; the inconsistencies are embarrassing.
But I know now I am not a freak; I'm a survivor whose been hurt terribly.

Two years later still in intensive therapy
She kept her promise, and we had no idea just how life could be.
As we heal--we see as the layers peel away
And realize why others would want to stay.
I'm just me today to the best of my ability--
Feeling however I feel--no matter what that may be.

Thank God for Bobby, my precious bro,
Who keeps my feelings out on the darkest of days, you know.
As even in healing--terror, despair, and pain so intense
At times doubt sets in whether to ever love, die, or just pretend.
But I've been dead for way too long and will not act no more--FOR NO ONE!
No more secrets, no more lies--
I'm not crazy after all--the truth inside of me arrives.

When I know how I feel on a given day, I be my feelings as Tammy says.
Then everything is okay 'cause I'm healing after all these years.
I'm living for me...as it should be...even with no one near.

When I'm able to be a feeling side of me, Tammy says let that be all of me.
Then I wonder if I'm real or not as I become aware who is out.
I feel scared and wonder *How can each be real?*
When I become aware of another's presence there.
Then I remember my other lives and doubt my existence at this time.

They each are real, she says, a part of me.
Right now I just let each be there no matter which side or how it feels.
I was never allowed to feel or the utter terror still.
As I heal and begin to feel, they all are separate--*from different worlds.*
Sometimes I wonder who am I? If they are all me as we heal, we become one still.
Yet, each was born to survive so which one is the *real me* and will remain alive?

I was thinking not long ago
No wonder others know how to be: It is no act--they're not *performing.*
When you feel, you just *be,* and everything flows accordingly.
So many people, so many lives, we've been broken too many times.
No more emotions frozen away 'cause we're all coming out to play.
We have a voice today--we're healing--we did not die.
We are so grateful to God we're alive!

SABOTAGE

IT USE TO LIVE INSIDE OF ME
    WITH SELF-HATRED AND DESPAIR.

TRYING TO PROTECT ME FROM EVERYTHING OUT THERE
    BUT ONLY DESTROYING ME AS LIFE GOING NOWHERE.

IT WAS BORN FROM ABUSE
    A LONG, LONG TIME AGO.

IT THINKS IT'S PROTECTING US
    FROM WHAT WE SHOULDN'T KNOW.

IT THINKS IF WE KNEW THE FACTS OF OUR PAST ACTUALITY
    THAT WE WOULD DIE FROM THE TRUTH OF ITS HORRENDOUS REALITY.

BUT AS WE HOWLED AND LET OUT SOME RAGE AND PAIN WITHIN,
    WE BROKE ITS WALL AND REALIZED IT IS JUST DENIAL THEN.

WE KNOW THE TRUTH OF OUR GOODNESS AND VALUE NOW.
    WE LET THE SELF-HATRED OUT OF US; NO LONGER IN DESPAIR.

WE GIVE IT ALL BACK TO YOU.
    WE MATTER; WE ALWAYS DID.

YOU TRANSFERRED ALL YOUR GUILT, SHAME, AND ANGER FOR YOUR SINS
    TO AN INNOCENT CHILD, WHO TOOK IT IN.

BUT NOW THAT CHILD HAS A VOICE AGAIN.
    IT IS NOT HER FAULT—IT WAS YOUR FAULT—IT ALWAYS HAD BEEN.

THEN I UNDERSTAND WHAT SAFETY MEANS.
    THERE IS LESS FEAR OF THE MEMORIES.

WHEN YOU KNOW YOU ARE NOT CRAZY,
    YOU'RE INTERNALLY READY TO FACE THE TRUTH: I'M A VALUABLE HUMAN BEING.

IT'S FROM A LONG TIME AGO,
    AND YOU ALREADY SURVIVED.

WHEN PEOPLE MADE YOU BELIEVE YOU WERE BAD,
    HURT YOU, AND YOU THOUGHT THAT YOU WOULD DIE.

SO YOU BURIED THE MEMORIES SO YOU WOULD NEVER KNOW,
    AND IT LIVED INSIDE AND CONTROLLED YOUR LIFE FROM THAT MOMENT ON.

YOU THOUGHT IF YOU REMEMBERED, IT WOULD KILL YOU;
    YET THE ONE THING YOU NEED IN RECOVERY IS THE TRUTH.

BUT IT'S A LOSING BATTLE IF YOU THINK IT WILL PUT AN END TO YOU
    BECAUSE YOU USE EQUIVALENT SURVIVAL STRENGTH TO KEEP IT BURIED AWAY,
    AND YOU WONDER WHY YOU'RE RUNNING IN PLACE EVERYDAY!

GETTING SCARED

EVERY NIGHT AFRAID TO GO TO BED;
FEAR WITH DREAD THIS NIGHT I'LL WET THE BED OR GET SCARED.
COMPLETE PANIC AND TERROR INSIDE;
WANNA RUN AND HIDE.
WISHING THAT SCARY FEELING WOULD GO AWAY;
TERRIFIED THAT YOU'RE CRAZY.
NO ESCAPE IN SIGHT
AS YOU'RE RUNNING FROM YOUR MIND.

BODY RUNNING THROUGH THE HOUSE FOR SAFETY;
SOMETIMES JUMPING UP ON THE SINK.
CROUCHED ON TWO LEGS LIKE AN ANIMAL AFRAID TO GET DOWN OR TOUCH THE GROUND.
SOMETHING BAD WILL HAPPEN TO YOU WITHOUT A DOUBT.
SCREAMING, CRYING, TALKING INCOHERENTLY TO HER THEN.
TRYING TO EXPLAIN AND MAKE SENSE OF WHAT'S HAPPENING.
NO ONE UNDERSTANDS AS YOU SHARE YOUR FEAR;
IT JUST MAKES YOU SOUND CRAZIER.

SHE TRIES TO CALM YOU DOWN;
GIVES YOU WATER AND TUCKS YOU IN.
SHE TELLS YOU THAT YOU ARE IMAGINING IT
AND THAT YOU ARE MAKING YOUR TUMMY SICK.
YOU TRY REALLY HARD NOT TO FEEL SICK
AND WONDER WHY YOU WOULD WANT TO BE SICK.

YOU ALWAYS WISHED THE MORNING AFTER
YOU REMEMBERED WHAT YOU WERE TRYING TO EXPLAIN THE NIGHT BEFORE TO HER.
NOW YOU NO LONGER KNOW WHAT WAS SO IMPORTANT TO YOU THEN.
AND IN THE MORNING, YOU ARE FILLED WITH SHAME.
NO LONGER REMEMBERING DETAILS OF THE NIGHT BEFORE
WHEN YOU TRIED TO TELL BUT NO ONE HEARD.

STOMACH ACHES, NAUSEA EXTREME.
WAITING TO THROW UP, BUT NOTHING SEEN.
WEAKNESS, FEAR, PANIC INSIDE
TRY TO USE THE BATHROOM BUT CAN'T STAY STILL AS YOU TRY TO SIT DOWN.

STAND UP, SIT DOWN--UP, DOWN, UP, DOWN, UP, DOWN--
'TILL SHE SLAPS YOU ACROSS THE FACE TO CALM YOU DOWN.
DAD SLEEPS OR TELLS YOU TO COUNT
WHICH TURNS AGAINST YOU AND BECOMES YOUR FEAR TOO.

YOU KNOW THAT NO ONE CAN HELP YOU
AS SHE CHASES YOU AROUND THE HOUSE AND YOU'RE HYSTERICAL.
SHE TELLS YOU IT'S ALL MADE UP INSIDE YOUR HEAD.
SHE GETS LIKE THAT TOO--YOU'RE HELPLESS.
THERE'S NOTHING YOU CAN DO--
'CAUSE EVEN MOMMY CAN'T HELP YOU--IT'S INSIDE OF YOU.
AT FIRST THEY LET YOU SLEEP WITH THEM
'TILL IT HAPPENS MORE OFTEN.

MANY TIMES WHEN YOU WOKE IN A SWEAT;
YOU SHOT STRAIGHT UP OUT OF BED.
YOU DIDN'T WANT TO BOTHER MOM;
SOMETIMES CALMED YOURSELF DOWN.
THE PRESSURE WITHIN LIKE THE REPETITIVE NITEMARES;
SWINGING BRANCH TO BRANCH WONDERING HOW LONG YOU COULD KEEP UP.
SO MUCH FRIGHT TO DO THE IMPOSSIBLE;
KNOWING YOU CAN'T YET CAN 'TIS NOT AN OPTION.

USUALLY WHEN IT CONTINUES TO ESCALATE;
YOU FEEL YOUR BODY BALLOONING--ESPECIALLY YOUR HAND--AND THINK OF DEATH.
GOD AND DEATH--HOW WOULD IT FEEL TO BE DEAD?
STUCK IN THE SKY STATIONARY WHILE EVERYTHING DOWN HERE KEPT GOING.

THAT THOUGHT TERRIFIES YOU;
SOMETIMES YOU GO TO THE BATHROOM.
DRINK WATER LIKE SHE ALWAYS GIVES YOU,
BUT YOUR REFLECTION SCARES YOU 'CAUSE IT DOESN'T LOOK LIKE YOU.

YOU DON'T LOOK NO MORE.
YOU STAND BY HER OPEN DOOR.
SHE WOULD FEEL YOU EVERY TIME.
SHE WOULD SAY: "IS THAT YOU, JULIE?"
YOU WOULD STAND REAL STILL;
NOT WANTING TO BOTHER HER STILL.
SHE WOULD TELL YOU TO "COME HERE."
SOMETIMES YOU WOULD BUT USUALLY YOU CAN'T STAY STILL AS IT'S GROWING WORSE.

MANY TIMES YOU WOULD START YOUR RUN THROUGHOUT THE HOUSE--
LITERALLY TERRIFIED AS SHE'D FOLLOW YOU AROUND AND TRY TO CALM YOU DOWN.
THIS WENT ON FOR YEARS IT SEEMS--
'TILL ONE DAY THEY STOPPED--I WAS SO RELIEVED.
I ALWAYS WONDERED AS YEARS WENT BY
WHY I GOT SCARED LIKE THAT AS A CHILD.
SO MANY STRANGE THINGS I EXPERIENCED WHEN YOUNG--
NOBODY I TOLD KNEW WHAT ANY OF IT MEANT.

I WAS GRATEFUL WHEN THEY STOPPED--
'TILL 15 YEARS LATER WHEN THEY CAME BACK.
I THOUGHT "OH MY GOD--THEY ARE BACK AGAIN"!
LIKE WHEN I WAS LITTLE, BUT NOW I'M NOT SAFE WHEN AWAKE EITHER.
THEN THE SEARCH FOR HELP BEGAN FOR THE NEXT 15 YEARS
AS MY LIFE BECAME UNBEARABLE TO LIVE.

TRUST

THE DAY EACH SIDE IS NOT ALIVE IN THE PAST;
THEIR BURIED LIFE RE-VISITED.
FROM DISTORTIONS TO CLARITY AND REALITY;
NO MORE CONFUSION OR LOSS OF IDENTITY.

EACH EMOTION FROZEN IN TIME;
LATER BROUGHT BACK TO LIFE.
EXPERIENCING ITS TRUTH AND ITS LIFE;
THEN BLENDING AND COMBINING INTO MINE.

TRUST WILL COME EASY THEN;
NO MORE CHAOS WITHIN.
WHICH VOICE TO LISTEN TO OR NOT;
ONE VOICE AND KNOWING THROUGHOUT.

WHO TO TRUST IN OUR WORLD NOW
WILL BE IMAGINABLE.
THAT WORLD FROM LONG AGO
WILL LIVE INSIDE OF US NO MORE.

GOD'S

PRESENCE

WHEN YOU FEAR YOU HAVE NO ONE,
AND YOU FEEL ALL ALONE.

WHEN THE PEOPLE IN YOUR LIFE,
HURT YOU, DISAPPOINT YOU, BETRAY YOU, LEAVE YOU, AND LIE.

WHEN THE HURT AND PAIN INSIDE HAS OVER-FLOWED TOO MANY TIMES,
TRUST SHATTERED; NO ONE LOOKS SAFE TO YOUR WEARY EYES.

WHEN THERE SEEMS LIKE NOTHING ELSE TO DO,
YOU LOOK TO GOD WHO, AT YOUR WORST, YOU FORGOT TO TURN TO.

THINKING HIS ARMS WERE NOT REAL ENOUGH;
DESIRING TOUCH OF A MAN TO HEAL YOUR ACHING HEART.

THOUGH DISCONNECTED AS YOU ARE,
IT ONLY INTENSIFIES THE LONELINESS AND ALIENATION BY FAR.

YET WHEN HIS LIGHT EMBRACES YOU,
IN AN INSTANT FLASH YOU FEEL THE TRUTH.

I AM NEVER ALONE--GOD IS ALWAYS WITH ME!
I NO LONGER *NEED* THE WRONG COMPANY.

I CAN GO ABOUT IN THIS LIFE PEACEFULLY;
GOD ALWAYS TAKES CARE OF ME AND MY NEEDS.

ONCE THE BLINK OF THIS WORLD DOES PASS;
I WILL LIVE ETERNALLY IN BLISS.

FREEDOM

Happiness is being how you feel freely expressed through

Peace of accepting who you are free-flowing to

Feel and live each moment of each day fluidly

Loving as you are free internally.

FEELING, ACCEPTING, LIVING, LOVING: *B E I N G.*

SELF-LOVE GROWING, VALUE SPREADING, LOVE RADIATING.

No longer looking for someone to make you feel *Complete.*

You are *Whole* internally.

Externals of life are a bonus once again

When you are *Free,* you are *Home* within.

CLUELESS EXISTENCE

The agony living inside of me;
Split lives for an eternity.
Looking good and oh so fine;
No one believing it is a survival lie.

Better off in my nitemares:
Bloody heap curled in a ball.
Crying and screaming at the top of my lungs.
No sound. I am mute. No voice at all.
Please help me! Someone hear me!
Please see me. I'm not well.
People just walk right by me like I'm crazy as hell.
Step over me--HOW DARE ME!
I am lying in the middle of the street--
Completely noticeable--a bloody heap.
Yet I am only a nuisance at their feet.

In a waking world, someone would notice that scene.
One pair of compassionate eyes could have saved me.
That never happened most my life.
I bleed all over the place; nobody perceives or tries.
Not with my waking face and articulate mouth;
Long sturdy legs and degrees on the wall.
No one saw under all my developed images;
Created to conceal buried memories forgotten.
Except with each new found enemy;
Further abuse to the dying me in a hidden heap unseen.

Everytime we feel, triggers everywhere become unbearable.
A split to another side who then takes over.
No one gets a good, long accurate look that tells a story.
We keep changing and seeming to cope magnificently.
Managing well others might add;
Yet, somewhere inside I am crying, *Please Come Back.*
That's not the truth.
A protector is talking to you.

When you inconspicuously slip to the front,
Who formerly left when a survivor came out.
No one knows what just took place;
They cannot discern by the look on your face.
Or they think you are playing games with their head;
You have long since come to believe that must be what's happening.
Yet, I cannot control them--they control me.
And who, if anybody, would ever believe me?

They may not have liked what they observed after you left.
You wish you could stay; pain grasped and witnessed.
Less than a quick glimpse of hidden wreckage seen
Before protection and strength became me.
Yet *I am going away, I'm gone--it's too late now.*
But I'm not--I just can't come out!
Screaming but mute: *Please don't go away!*
Help me--I need you to stay.
Something's wrong with me.
I can't go on living this way.

No one knows when you are gone,
As they think that you are ONE.
Who else could you be;
They judge you as they so conceive.
No other truth exists in their minds;
Reality to them is one body--one life.

You are treated as ONE so many times;
Wishing you could make sense of your life.
Feeling most the time how bad that you are
Yet bouncing around like a ping pong ball.
Making enemies with your numerous perceptions;
Distorted eyes from a life of misery forgotten.

Many lives switching all over the place--
Stay away from people, relationships, good that comes my way.
After years and no help with your chaotic existence,
You decipher the patterns and become more co-conscious.
Your sides will keep anyone you love away.
The closer you become, they won't let you stay.

Beautiful eyes to those gazing your image.
The world seeing your strength, your ambition.
Physically fit in appearance;
A runner so disciplined.
Determination and perseverance;
Healthy living to their vision.

They have no clue who you are and what it is like;
You don't even understand what the hell is happening inside.
Doctors can't even figure you out;
Life without hope most the time without a doubt.
Projecting your world onto everyone you meet;
Believing your insanity.
You are triggered;
It remains your reality.

Whenever you get to come back for a while;
You are better off gone as your life is in shambles.
Whatever was going on when you left;
It is not always the same, and you know it's your fault.
And whomever you began to get close to before;
Destruction has put an end to it all.
Many lives you live each day
Wondering what it would be like to live in *another* for one day.

Begin once again to put your life back together.
By now, knowing your system--fearing the endless cycle.
Every time you build your life to a desirable place;
It all goes away, and you are left running in place.
Beginning to grasp how many times can I start all over again
As I observe in the end, I just cannot win!
Confused, scared, and unaware most my life--
Wondering what I've done this time—just trying desperately to survive.
Programmed Computer with no memory;
Completely clueless to the existence inside of me.

FROM LIFE
TO DEATH

FIRST CAME THE NEED AND DESIRE FOR LOVE;

THEN THE PAIN AND TERROR WE SPLIT FROM.

DESPERATION AND SEDUCTION SURVIVE FOR A TIME;

ANOTHER FILLED WITH HATE AND RAGE INSIDE.

LEFT WITH SHAME AND FEAR ONCE AGAIN;

GONE AS ETERNAL DESPAIR AND DOOM SET IN.

THE NEED
** UNCONDITIONAL LOVE **

LOVE FREELY GIVEN BUT NOT RETURNED.
ONE DAY TO DIE AND BECOME FROZEN.
NEVER GO TO THE PLACE WHERE IT HURTS.
NOT AN OPTION BURIED UNDER LAYERS OF GUNK.
SOMEHOW AWARE ENOUGH TO KNOW IT EXISTS.
JUST NEVER GO THERE AS IT EQUALS DEATH.

NO MAN, NO SEX, NO CHOICE AT ALL.
LATER ONE MAN REACHES THE LOVE.
AN ENDLESS, BOTTOMLESS PIT OF NEED THERE.
NEVER LET IT BE SEEN EVER!
ESSENTIAL TO SURVIVAL THAT I DIED WITHOUT.
YET INTERNALLY LOVE SURVIVED SOME HOW.

SPENT A LIFETIME IN TERROR.
YEARS--GRIEVING, ACHING, CRYING, AND RAGING.
YOU MUST ENTER THE LOVE TO HEAL THE PAIN.
ENTER EACH SIDE FROZEN WITHIN.
SOMEDAY I HIT THE BOTTOM OF THE PIT
AND IF STILL ALIVE, I AM FREE TO LIVE.

AN UNSAFE WORLD

IN THE COMPANY OF OTHERS
MY BODY REFLEXIVELY TIGHTENS AND BREATHING BECOMES SHALLOW.
PANIC CONSUMES ME; I CAN'T THINK OR BREATHE AT ALL.
I HAVE LIVED THIS WAY SO CHRONICALLY, IT HAS BECOME NORMAL.

I LEAVE MY BODY WHEN PEOPLE APPROACH;
DON'T TALK TO ME OR LOOK AT ME OR GET TOO CLOSE.
EVEN WHEN I AM ALL ALONE,
I GO AWAY TO THE PLACE WHERE IT DOESN'T HURT SO MUCH.
ONLY NOW REALIZING JUST HOW OFTEN I'M GONE;
HOW LITTLE TIME I'VE SPENT IN MY BODY ALL ALONG.

MY LIFE KEEPS CHANGING TO PROTECT ME I KNOW.
YET ONLY REALLY HURTS ME AND LEAVES ME ALONE.
MORE AND MORE PEOPLE FILTER THROUGH MY LIFE;
I CAN'T GET TOO CLOSE, TERROR INSIDE.

THE SYSTEM GETS RID OF THE ONES WE CAN'T TRUST.
CONNECTION KEEPS LESSENING--NO ONE PASSES OUR TEST.
THE MOST IMPORTANT THING TO A SENSITIVE PERSON LIKE ME
TAKEN FROM MY LIFE SO EARLY.
THE MORE I DESIRE PEOPLE AND LOVE--IT'S NO USE.
THE STRONGER THEY WORK TO ELIMINATE YOU.
A LIFETIME OF ISOLATION, ALIENATION, CONFUSION, TERROR, AND PAIN.
INABILITY TO MAINTAIN HEALTHY RELATIONSHIPS TIME AND AGAIN.

ALCOHOL BECAME MY ONLY SAVIOR
ATTEMPTING TO REPRESS WHAT WE COULD CONTAIN NO LONGER.
WHEN LOVE WAS TRIGGERED, ALL THE LITTLE ONES BEGAN TO UNFREEZE
TRIGGERED ALL OVER THE PLACE FROM INSIDE OF ME.
THE INSANITY OF MY LIFE AS IT BEGINS TO UNFOLD
MADE LIVING NEARLY IMPOSSIBLE.

EVEN THAT DRINK DIDN'T HELP FOR LONG.
FOOLED WHO I THOUGHT WAS THE IMPORTANT WORLD
WHILE IT BROUGHT MY WORTH TO ZERO.
INABILITY TO BE AROUND ANYONE WITHOUT A DRINK.
AFTER A LIFETIME OF TERROR AND SYMPTOMS, AGORAPHOBIC IS ME.

NOW I AM ADDICTED TO ALCOHOL
TO ESCAPE THE FEELINGS FROM CHILDHOOD.
ADDITIONAL SHAME FOR MY SOLITARY WAYS
PILED AND LAYERED ON TOP OF MY DEEPLY ROOTED SHAME.
ANYTHING I DO AND EVERYWHERE I GO--
WHOEVER I MEET--ESPECIALLY THOSE I KNOW.
ALL IS A TRIGGER TO A FEELING SIDE OF ME
THAT IS COMPLETELY OVERWHELMED IN AGONY.

THEY HAVE BEEN FROZEN IN TIME MOST MY LIFE.
WHAT CONTROL COULD NO LONGER CONTAIN INSIDE.
AS THE LITTLE ONES BEGAN TO COME OUT,
WORKING AND BEING FUNCTIONAL WAS IMPOSSIBLE.
THE DOOR MUST CLOSE ALL THE WAY;
NO MORE FEELINGS AT ALL THIS WAY.

REALITY AT WORK BECOMES CLEAR RIGHT AWAY.
PEOPLE TRIGGER FEELINGS AND THE DOOR OPENS SOME DAYS.
LOSS OF JOBS, INTIMACY, AND PEOPLE LEFT AND RIGHT.
INSANITY IN MOTION OR I'M DEAD ALL THE TIME!

ONLY BY THE GRACE OF GOD,
STRONG WILL AND STRENGTH I PUSH ON.
DETERMINATION OF STEEL AND PERSEVERANCE OF TEN;
I DON'T KILL MYSELF FROM THE BATTLE WITHIN.
LOOK FINE AND APPEAR NORMAL;
THE FUCKING WALKING DEAD FOR SURVIVAL.

DEAD BUT ALIVE AND FUNCTIONING FOR LESSER AND LESSER DEGREES.
BECOMING PHYSICALLY MORE AND MORE PARALYZED.
WONDERING WHAT IS GOING TO HAPPEN TO ME?
NO LONGER ACCESS TO FEELINGS AT ALL--
DARKNESS TAKES OVER--MY LIFE IS AN ANAL BLACK HOLE.
NOT BELIEVING I CAN GO ON ANY LONGER LIKE THIS;
YET ANY LONGER GOES ON FOR MANY YEARS.
SOME HOW, SOME WAY I AM STILL HERE.

GOD REVEALED TO ME THE TRUTH OF THIS WORLD.
AT THOSE ENDING MOMENTS, HE WOULDN'T LET ME GO.
I CAME TO UNDERSTAND IN REVERENCE TO HIM AND MY BRO,
I COULD NOT LET THEM DOWN AS THEY BOTH LOVE ME SO.
GOD KNEW THERE WOULD BE A DAY IN THE FUTURE;
I WOULD NOT ONLY SURVIVE BUT THRIVE AND HAVE A PURPOSE.
THAT DAY IS APPROACHING BY THE MIRACLE OF TAMMY,
AND MANY GIFTS GOD PLACED HERE WHEN DEATH WAS UPON ME.

ARE MY SIDES

SABOTAGE OR PROTECTION?

ROSE KEEPS US FROM COMING OUT SO WE DO NOT BOUNCE AROUND.

VICKY KEEPS US FROM HAVING ANYBODY ELSE AROUND.

VERONICA KEEPS US STRONG AND FAR FROM FEELING SO WE CAN GO ON LIVING.

JOE KEEPS US FROM FEAR AND CLOSENESS AS HER FOCUS IS ON SELF--NOT OTHERS.

MARGARET KEEPS US IN TERROR AND SHAME SO CAN'T FACE NO ONE OR DO NOTHING.

SANDY KEEPS US FROM BEING INTIMATE BY SEDUCTIVE HYSTERIA.

CINDY KEEPS US DESIRING LOVE AND LIFE.

MORE MEMORIES HERE?

JUJU KEEPS US AWAY FROM EXTREME PAIN BY GOING SOME PLACE SAFE.

SABOTAGE KEEPS US IN CONTINUAL TURMOIL AND CONFUSION SO WE DON'T REMEMBER.

SAM KEEPS US FROM WANTING TO LIVE AS HE DOESN'T BELIEVE WE DESERVE LIFE.

SALLY KEEPS US FROM LOVING AS SHE IS SELF-SUFFICIENT AND NEEDS NO ONE.

JWK KEEPS US FROM DEPENDENT NEED AND TEACHES US TO GIVE LOVE HEALTHILY.

HEALING

DESPAIR CAME FIRST, THEN THE SCREAMS

UNLEASHING THE RAGE THAT STRUCK THE PAIN

AND TERROR LIVING INSIDE OF ME.

AND UNDERNEATH, IN MISERY,

LIES MORE HURT, FEAR, AND

BURIED MEMORIES.

UMBILICAL CORD
RELEASE

From pain, ache, and guilt inside
To freedom, love, and life.
A lifetime of co-dependency and enmeshment;
Learned through taking care of a mother and brother.

Being responsible for emotions of others besides me;
Never allowed or had time to know my own needs.
Whenever you love someone deeply within,
Expression of love triggers unresolved pain.

Avoidance becomes more desirable then--
As you connect love to pain and ache within.
Amazing release not long ago;
When I cried and I screamed out more hurt from my mother.

I drove around in my car after church;
Letting the pain inside re-surface.
How she hurt me too many times to keep count,
And I'm responsible for making her happy some how.

A brother who became like a son as Mom in pain and overwhelmed;
Hence, my sister and I became like mini-mothers.
All I know is that for years I've been carrying this pain;
Anyone I love strikes the need once again.

The need for unconditional love I never received,
And a father who was taken away from me.
So the few who reach my heart touch the love turned enmeshment,
And the pain, need, and guilt tears me apart again.

I have known nothing different than love with pain,
But I recently experienced a significant release.
Compiled on top of her hurt that was always my fault;
I never experienced boundaries at all.

I cried out again the hurt and pain trapped inside;
From loving a mother who hurt me each time.
But this time I shouted out and named my pain,
And where it originated and processed same.

To learn to never let anyone know you hurt--
As the point is they did it on purpose.
I truly believe she loved me deeply,
But she had no recovery to make her stop hurting me.

A mother who left her, life in an orphanage,
An abusive father, and a husband who neglected her.
As I realized it is all in the past,
I let it go, I gave it back.

I cried and let out the pain trapped within
Of a little girl who hurt badly over and over again.
Now I feel the umbilical cord detach.
I feel free loving--less pain attached.

It doesn't mean I don't care or don't feel.
Like I can love my brother deeply--it just doesn't hurt now.
It's like a boundary has been created within.
He's on one side--me another--there's a separation.

So now when he's happy or hurting that I must take him back;
It's okay because I am not enmeshed.
I can operate from a place of knowing within
Understanding when his behavior means I must take action.

Instead of projecting my unresolved pain onto him.
Wondering and worrying *Is someone hurting him?*
At times, believing my pain was about him;
Thus, taking appropriate action based on that assumption.

But now I am changed, and I can feel the difference;
Since we are not umbilical corded together.

BECOMING
CO-CONSCIOUS

From blindness to vision;
   I'm becoming more present.
I am seeing and hearing and noticing things--
   People's expressions and voices and body language around me.
I am becoming aware of how they react in response to me.
   I am putting together which side's behavior that may be.
Although I feel strange as I become aware who I am;
   A thought came to me that this is where *normal* begins.
The more that I comprehend who is out;
   The more I understand how the little ones' react.
If my sides are just emotions split in time;
   Then my sides and emotions will soon combine.
Like Tammy once said over a year ago:
   Do your sides know each other? I just didn't know.
Now as I am becoming more present each day,
   I am getting to know my sides and how they behave.
How do you ever understand any different
   Than your own reality you assume normal?
Until years and years of consecutive pain;
   Patterns and people and you don't quite fit in.
Although through the years I began to know my system,
   Today I had a more clear glimpse of awareness.
In order to heal and be present each day,
   I must comprehend how I behave.

I had this feeling if my sides are just emotions frozen away,

    The more they are out, I am feeling today.

Recently, I became aware my sides are not always out;

    I'm living in survival mode still.

That is why it seems easier to cope;

    It's not that I'm so much better, I'm just not feeling at all.

When I am feeling more often each day, no wonder it is light.

    As I began to learn, feeling is living and that creates life.

No wonder three years ago, stickies kept being placed on the mirror.

    They were to remind us to KEEP FEELING no matter the fear.

Someone inside became conscious for a time

    And wanted us to have a life.

Knowing some how feeling was impossible;

    Yet we did for a time 'til life became unbearable.

The more that I become aware of the little ones' behavior;

    I can understand the transition from one to another.

Bring them into therapy, so each can tell its story.

    It amazes me how bad that it was; I could not be present at all.

No wonder my memory of growing up always had the same old ring:

    I was always in trouble it seemed.

I didn't quite understand why; I was in confusion most the time.

    Life long since gone for an eternity, survival was my only means.

All the little ones created inside to help us stay alive.

    Split lives protected the child, but as an adult it's an insanity cycle.

Continue to get to know my sides and regain cooperation of their lives.

    The more the transition begins to blend, I will become more whole again.

STATE OF CONFUSION

Always in a state of confusion--
 Not quite sure if it is real or a delusion.
Comprehension that this is what you do.
 This is how you act, how you get, and others' perception of you.

Acceptance the key to your everyday life.
 So you can surrender without hate inside.
Understanding everything is exactly as it should be,
 I can love me at every moment of each day with a little peace.

Over and over and over again,
 Repetitive comments or statements or looks are given:

You don't seem like yourself. Now that's more like you. You're back to your normal self. You sound different today. You sound young. How old are you? That's outa character for you. You seem different. You're like two different people. You contradict yourself. Who am I talking to? I wouldn't want to get you mad. How can you switch on a dime like that? What did I do? I'm on your side. You've gotta trust somebody. Nobody's fucking with you! It's me-- I'm on your side. I miss youuuuuuuuuuu. I don't feel you. Why do you do that? Stop talking like that. Why do you act like that? What was that all about? What just happened here? I thought I knew you. You changed. This isn't the Julie I know. You're moody. Call me when you're in the right mood. You're so changeable. You liked doing that last week. Nothing changed--you changed. Why did you make plans if you don't want to? What changed? Are you okay? I've never seen this side of you before. You seem different. What's the matter with you? You're a sick puppy. You need intense help. Somebody messed with you bad. Did something happen to you? You're different now than when I met you. I want you to be the way you use to be. You're cute when you act like that. You're a great interviewer. I feel like I'm with somebody else. You're my rough, tough cream puff. Don't play games with me. I'm tired of your games. How come yesterday you cranked out work and today you can't do anything right? I know you're not stupid so why are you acting that way now? I wasn't born yesterday! Don't lie to me! You knew how to do that last week! How come you don't remember attorneys and clients-- you were talking on the phone with her before lunch? We're gonna start calling you the post-it girl. Don't write it--just listen. You can't write everything down--some things you have to remember. That's the main character in the movie--haven't you been watching!? Stop playing stupid with me. You act like a little kid sometimes. Grow up. Act your age. So self-conscious. You're so pure, I wanna corrupt you. I just answered that question; weren't you listening? Pay attention. Focus. I'm talking to you--Hello, do you hear me? Look at me. Where are you? I just told you that. You're not thinking. Space cadet. Airhead. How could you not remember that? You should know this. How can you not notice that? Something's wrong with your memory. Do you smoke pot? How come you can recite things verbatim and yet you can't even remember what I just told you? You already met me, remember? You're weird. You're a goob. You sound different. Your voice sounds completely different on my voicemail than your earlier message. Did I wake you? She's always been like that. That's just Julie. You make me laugh. You're funny. She always does that. You're repeating yourself. You already told me that. You should already know that. How could you not see that!? Don't you remember anything I tell you? We already went over that. Don't you remember? Why do you play stupid all the time? How could you miss that sign? How come after you put on your face, you act different? Watch--she'll be late, and then she'll act different. Come back, Julie. I want the old Julie back. Will the real Julie please come out? Julie, come back. Who am I talking to? You're not being your self today.

How many other things have I been told or strange expressions given?
    Things I have heard said in my presence not quite comprehending?
Except it is somehow me again--
    As I try to figure out what I did or missed and observe patterns.
No doctors can figure me out.
    Maybe I have a hearing problem or am A.D.D. some how.
Yet, I am told my hearing is just fine.
    I am checked out for A.D.D. this time.
Trying to find a label for what is wrong inside!

I miss big enough chunks out of movies all over the place.
    I am always confused like there's this big joke everyone gets, and I miss.
Dan thought I was faking it or playing stupid all the time.
    Since I knew I wasn't faking it, I must not be too bright.
Yet my stupidity even fluctuates in time.
    My intelligence has been demonstrated and reflected by others in my life.
However, it would make sense of my whole life it seems,
    Except Mom always said how smart that I happened to be.
But *smart* didn't seem like a good thing coming from her--
    As she compared me to my aunt at those raging moments.

How come I don't remember important parts of movies?
    I thought I was paying attention as it is important to me.
Besides, the only thing to do at a movie is WATCH THE MOVIE.
    So something must be wrong with me.
But the A.D.D. doctor told me I passed the test with flying colors.
    So now there is no way I'm A.D.D. either!
He said the symptoms are related to something else.
    That was the final straw that snapped.

So I don't have a hearing problem. I am not stupid or have A.D.D.
    I have been in terror all my life. No one can help me.
No doctors can figure me out.
    Medications and other diagnoses have not fixed me.

Everywhere I go and everything I see--
     Everything I do--something is happening to me--I'm not imagining.
Doctors and men I've ever known all my life
     Keep asking me if I was sexually abused at one time.
I kept saying *no* as I remembered very little.
     How do you know you don't remember what you don't remember?

Depending on who is out--
     Each side holds separate memories and feelings you forgot.
When you change or switch to another side,
     Those feelings and memories go completely from your life.
Until you return again not knowing what just happened.
     But then, of course, this has been your only reality.
You're hardly gone for months at a time--
     More like days, minutes, and seconds of your life.
Confusing others not understanding your time lost;
     Most sides have amnesia for the other sides' time out.
Those sides who hold the terror and memories most damaging to you--
     They hardly come out at all and share your past truth.
Instead they come out and behave in manners unlike you--
     Acting out, yet sabotaging, to protect you from the truth.
As they live inside you distorting your view,
     While somewhere inside a *Watcher* wonders what the hell is happening to you.

I tried going to a survivor meeting years before, but I couldn't stop crying.
     Didn't like how I felt when I left, so I stopped going.
I decided to try and go back to a survivor meeting again.
     Especially when sexual abuse around me sent me childhood symptoms.
From the moment I set foot in the meeting in Costa Mesa, **I was home.**
     Someone understood my symptoms, my body sensations, and my life.
Everything no other doctor or person could explain,
     Except to look at me with a dumbfounded look like I'm strange!

The A.D.D. doctor did say this, and I remember.
     You've been operating for so long under a high level of anxiety.
When you slow down,
     Your brain slows considerably.
No wonder I have existed busy, busy, busy.
     To slow down I would feel my feelings or go away completely.
That makes sense now in therapy with Tammy.
     She is the only Psychologist who has been able to help me.
All my life I've been dissociating--I keep going away.
     So no wonder I don't remember or understand things all over the place!!

MIRACLE SYSTEM

The more I heal the more I'm baffled by unimaginable truth.
I should be dead but by the grace of God I'm still here.
I'm a complete and utter miracle that words alone can not discern.
I not only survived--my system maintained a somewhat *normal* existence.

My life for the most part appeared *fine*.
Instead of reflecting the complete and utter destruction inside.
What a system inside of me--I love them all so completely.
Amazing the strength inside them all.
Unbelievable yet I'm grasping undeniably real.
We survived formidable devastation from so long ago.

Unfolding truth as my eyes begin to clear.
Life surviving death with amazing mastery.
Splitting and switching in everyday life.
Coming out some how through the years *fine*.

It so amazes me still as I comprehend the wreckage in here.
Because of its burial so magnificently done
To the point it never existed at all.
Yet actually understanding the magnitude that it did.
System working overtime to keep us in check.

I'm walking through and healing what was done--
Knowing I am a miraculous child of God.
Awareness that this is how poets or writers create such work.
It is like you go way beyond the place of death or exterior limits.
Those who endure have a story and great purpose.
By the grace of God, I am a survivor still.

Another glimpse of how safety feels.
When you KNOW it's from a long ago world.
Where you no longer live the majority of time.
Where you survived insurmountable odds and are alive.

It is living inside of you terrifying you still.
Some how, some way you can remember though.
More separate because you know the truth:
I'm not crazy, I have value, and safety too.

I'm alive because my system took care of me
In unspeakable ways blowing the walls off reality.
When I get a glimpse of the size of that truth,
I wish I could express words to articulate IT'S HUGE.

How many times she looks so normal.
She has a professional job.
She seems fine in this world.
She has no clue--her system keeps protecting her.
She seems to adapt well to the point NO ONE KNOWS OR CARES.

She vacillates between needing HELP and insanity.
She is not co-conscious enough to grasp her reality!
She is triggered all over the place.
Symptoms that she somehow copes with each day.
LIMITED LIFE that she is use to and must face.

NO ONE NOTICES THE DEGREE OF HELP SHE NEEDS.
Other people can't quite put it together, you see.
How BIG IT IS all over the place.
Except for maybe the men who get close.
BUT THEN THEY'RE GONE--she needs no one at all.

Like that movie:
It's so nice to have you back to your OLD self again.
As she smiles meekly, *Thanks.*
Then she looks straight into the camera clueless.
Yet somewhere inside eyes computing a flicker of recognition.
Yet coming up empty just as quickly--never quite registering.
Not enough consciousness to put words to her reality!
LIVING A COMPLETELY BAFFLED, CONFUSED LIFE IN ACTUALITY.

My sides are layered on top of the memories.
Doing anything to keep the memories from surfacing.
PROTECTION YET SABOTAGE protecting the life of me.
They believe remembering would kill me.
Until Sam's wall burst, and I didn't die.
NOW I CAN REMEMBER AND HAVE A LIFE!

No wonder it's so difficult to heal.
System so seemingly complex and adaptive.
Protecting self yet no memory recall.
To acknowledge the switch--the systems on call.
You just go through life bouncing like a ping pong ball.

Not knowing what the HELL is wrong with you.
How can you get better if you can't catch more than a glimmer of truth?
Symptoms are impossible to bear.
You spend life just trying to survive everywhere.
Clean up after all the messes in your world.
With only years of patterns you are learning to decipher.

That's why they call us survivors I told my friend as I scream.
Because IT IS SO HARD NOT TO GIVE UP WITH ALL THIS UNBEARABLE PAIN!
The odds are against us surviving the original abuse.
Then NOT TO GIVE UP WITH LOW SELF WORTH, PROJECTED VALUE, AND
SYMPTOMS.
TO NOT JUST KILL YOURSELF OR END UP IN PRISON!

Your strong denial system keeps the truth buried layers below.
It thinks the truth unleashed and revealed would kill you all.
So everytime you get close to a memory, you feel more insanity.
Because at the moment you split, you would have died from the pain.
So the system keeps it buried away so you can survive another day.
Yet you are trying to heal as life surviving is no longer endurable.
To break through those walls and function at all--
THOSE WHO SURVIVE ARE A FUCKING MIRACLE!

The miracle and insanity of other personalities.
They made childhood bearable but adulthood a merry-go-round of confusion.
Running in terror from the closest to healthy love I've known.
Love and closeness has always been impossible.
It must be the ultimate mind fuck and betrayal.
The closer you get to touching the root love inside you.
The stronger the defenses and sides work to keep you away.
Because it is right next door to the original love
Before I became we and life became death.

FLUID EMOTIONS
(Short Version)

A glimpse into another world where feelings flow to and fro.
Fluid like a forgotten day when emotions were free to come out and play.

Life will once again be free, feeling and being all of me.
Smooth transitions side to side neither frozen nor compartmentalized.

Eloquently swirling amid varying colors inconsistent.
Beauty and peace so completely existing.

When such a glimpse comes my way, I hold to the memory, I'm healing today.
As I switch from side to side, I grasp I'm not living another life.

As I heal, I'm becoming free, every single part of me.
Soon not going to the OTHER side but accessing ME as ONE life.

Fluttering feelings anew each day, never wandering a moment ahead.
Trusting the outcome just BEING brings, so freeing a life should be.

Fluid emotions so many lives behind you.
Unseen tracks more like traces by now.

Trapped inside, moments of expression when terror and pain your only lesson.
You forgot you knew a far off day when you could come out and play.

Then a moment reminds you of a life you thought you dreamed.
It all makes sense: This is the way it's supposed to be!

A time when life, the ebb and flow, once so normal and known.
Before they took it all away, and you forgot you knew another way.

More and more as you see light, you hope the dream may be right.
Not a flicker, a flash untrue, of a stolen life taken from you.

Out of the tunnel: Seeing and hearing and knowing it's me.
Fluid emotions more consistent and free.

In and out and to and from
All spontaneous feelings as We become One.

CONTROL

GOOD AND BAD ALL TWISTED AROUND.

IF YOU COME TO RELY ON HIM, HE'LL LET YOU DOWN.

LIKE HE WANTS YOU TO TRUST HIM.

HE KNOWS WHEN YOU DO--THEN BOOM!--HE GETS YOU.

BUT, BAMM!, I DON'T.   I NEVER DID.

HE CAN'T STAND THAT.   HE NEEDS CONTROL TO STAY IN TACT.

I NEEDED HIM ONCE BUT NEVER AGAIN.

DEPENDENT CHILD GRIEVING THE LOSS OF A DAD.

I HATE HIM--BUT I DON'T.

I LOVE HIM--BUT I DON'T.

I JUST GRIEVE AND LET HIM GO.

A FATHER WHOM IMAGE IS MOST IMPORTANT.

UNCONDITIONAL LOVE NONEXISTENT.

YOU ONLY GET THAT FROM THE FUCKING CRAZY MONSTER.

WHO LOVES YOU BUT IS JEALOUS OF YOUR FATHER.

A MOTHER WHO WAS BEATING ON YOU.

A FATHER WHO CLAIMED HE NEVER KNEW.

EVERYTIME YOU FEEL, IT IS NEVER ALLOWED.

IT IS SOME HOW A JOKE AS NOTHING TO HIM IS PERSONAL.

IF YOU THINK YOU HURT THERE, ONE OF HIS FAVORITE JOKES WENT:

HE'LL HIT YOUR BIG TOE WITH A HAMMER SO YOU WILL FORGET.

NOT COMPREHENDING THE PAIN DIDN'T GO AWAY.

A NEW PAIN TO PILE ON TOP OF OLD PAIN BURIED AWAY.

DOESN'T HE GET THAT'S WHAT OUR LIFE WAS REALLY LIKE?

FOCUS YOUR ATTENTION ON THE WORST PAIN AT ONE TIME.

PAIN EVERYWHERE YET INSIGNIFICANT TO EXPRESS IN OUR LIFE.

BOBBY CAN'T EVEN EXPRESS IN WORDS.

JUST FRUSTRATION, RAISED HANDS, AND DISTURBED LOOKS.

HE AS AN <u>INDIVIDUAL</u> DOESN'T WANT TO DO AS DAD SAYS.

DAD JUST THREATENS AND USES CONTROL EVERYDAY.

IF YOU DON'T DO WHAT I JUST TOLD YOU TO DO,

I'LL TAKE THAT TOY OR THOSE HEADPHONES FROM YOU.

HE NEVER CONSIDERS HIS HUMAN <u>FEELINGS</u>.

NO CHOICES OR OPTIONS JUST DICTATING.

HE DISHES OUT DISCIPLINED LAWS AND RULINGS.

MAKING IT APPARENT HE HAS MUCH UNEXPRESSED GRIEF.

HIS MOTHER AND HIM BOTH NEED OTHERS' REACTIONS.

A LIFETIME OF REPRESSED ANGER HAS BEEN THEIR EXISTENCE.

OTHERS' <u>FEELINGS</u> TRIGGER THEIR DISOWNED REFLECTIONS.

MOM FREAKING OUT KEPT DAD FROM EVER SEEING HIMSELF.

YOU NEVER LEARN YOU OR YOUR NEEDS MATTER.

IF THEY DID WHY WOULD HE LET ABUSE HAPPEN?

<u>WHEN YOU FEEL</u>, YOU <u>CAN'T</u> STAND BY AND DO NOTHING AT ALL.

THAT'S NOT AN OPTION--IT'S IMPOSSIBLE!

TO LET HER DAD WHO ABUSED HER AND HE KNEW

WATCH US AND TAKE CARE OF US TOO!

YOUR ONE DAUGHTER IS FREAKING OUT EVERY NIGHT.

HE'S DAILY AT OUR HOUSE AND IN OUR LIVES

CALLING ME A DEVIL ALL THE TIME.

YOU GET HOME FROM GAMBLING,

HOW COULD YOU NOT HAVE A CLUE?

YOUR SEXUALLY ABUSED WIFE'S FATHER

SEPARATED YOUR DAUGHTERS IN DIFFERENT ROOMS?!

UNLESS YOU STOPPED FEELING SOMEWHERE IN TIME,

SO HOW CAN YOU IDENTIFY AND HAVE PERCEPTIONS OF OUR LIFE?

AS YOU EXPRESS ANGER OR FEELINGS IN DAILY LIVING AT ALL,

HE KEEPS ADDING TO YOUR RESTRICTIONS WHEN YOU OPEN YOUR MOUTH.

HE HAS YOU SIT IN A CHAIR AND SHUT UP FOR A WHILE.

TEACHING YOU MANY TIMES YOUR FEELINGS DON'T MATTER, SO YOU'RE MUTE NOW.

NOWHERE TO GO WITH ALL THESE UNEXPRESSED, BOILING FEELINGS.

BESIDES TO INTERNALIZE THEM ALL AT SOME POINT.

BELIEVING YOU'RE JUST A SPOT ON THE WALL.

YOU REALLY DON'T MATTER--YOU'RE NOT WORTHY AT ALL.

SO AS TIME GOES BY, WHY WOULD YOU TELL?

NO POWER TO YOU EVER REFLECTED BY HIM EVER.

YOUR EXISTENCE MEANS NOTHING, YOU ARE POWERLESS.

THE MOTHER ABUSING YOU IS THE ONLY ONE WHO LOVES.

HE'S A STRANGER THAT CONTROLS YOU AND DOESN'T EXIST AT ALL.

THE WAR ZONE
(Childhood with Mom and Dad)

Good and bad all twisted around.
If you come to rely on him, he'll let you down.
Like he wants you to trust him; He knows when you do.
Then BOOM!—He gets you. But, BAMM I don't. I never did.
He can't stand that. He needs control to stay in tact.

I needed him once but never again.
Dependent child grieving the loss of a dad.
I hate him—but I don't.
I love him—but I don't.
I just grieve and let him go.

A father whom image is most important.
Unconditional love nonexistent.
You only get that from the fucking crazy monster
Who loves you but is jealous of your father.

He pays no attention to her needs or her rage.
While he goes about his day, she attacks you in hate.
For all his neglect or useless attempts to make her stop once again.
Buries his head in the sand all over the place.
That's all he knows how to do having no father who placed value on him.
And a Mother with repressed emotions.

Meanwhile your daughter is trying to keep peace.
Knowing mom's got dad beat.
If she can just be a good little girl,
Mommy will be happy and love her still.
But Mommy can't stand her most of the time.
Takes daddy away from his daughter—she's left with no father.

Then one day in a miracle flash,
Daughter loses all feelings for her Dad.
The good news is she don't need him no more
'Till years later when she is going through hell.
Loving and needing what you can't have was too much to bear
For a little daughter whose father was everything to her.

More than anything she wanted mommy happy
Because she loved her—SENSITIVE CHILD THAT SHE HAPPENED TO BE.
There was no real choice living an unbearable situation.
Giving him up seemed the only solution.
She somehow knows their fights are about her
'Cause I'm just like her, Mommy says, when she was a little girl.

Mommy never healed as daddy enabled her monstrosity to grow
While all along he played out his martyr role.
The horrendous childhood abuse she lived through.
And nobody cared to save her and see the truth.

It was like looking in a mirror she saw reflected through me
The goodness of her inner being.
She never healed and never believed she was worthy.
She was on a mission to destroy anything loving perceived.
All that reminded her of herself who she hated ferociously still.

She'd say "Bob, who does she remind you of?" when I was silly.
Yet, she don't want daddy to pay attention to me.
So what I needed was taken away from me.
A DADDY WHO DIDN'T EVEN FIGHT FOR ME!
And he can't say he didn't know
As later in a therapy session, HE TOLD ME SO!

He's great at telling everyone else just how to be.
Yet his own eyes don't search within to change himself, you see.
Then he'd have to see emotions he chooses not to see
And look at who brainwashed who in our family.
That is why he chose mom as his wife to be.
He could hide behind her wounds and come out clean!

Once feelings are gone there is no life in her—she's gone.
Now she can survive her childhood that with feelings was impossible.
Years go by, and she tries to go on pretending she's fine.
When all along she's dead inside.
Wishing things could be the way they use to be—
Not quite understanding what that would be—some how a happy family.

She spends her life trying to act like a daughter would act with a dad.
When she feels nothing—has not a clue—he's always been a stranger to her.
She can't tell no one something happened to her 'cause she loves him.
Just like her Mommy's happiness being more important to her.
Not hurting his feelings—a burden she can't share and must bear alone.
As abuse continues to go on and on, she needs an outlet—something's wrong.
She tells her mom vaguely one day who only rages and slaps her around—
The typical medicine in our house.
Then the fairy tale ending as mommy goes from monster to loving.
Then I'm suppose to love her real fast before she gets mad and attacks.
I want to love her but I just can't switch emotions like that.
Never allowed to feel my pain for loving her as she became mean.

Daughter never tells another soul until her best friend in high school.
Now mom actually begins to hate her more as she's not reacting no more.
She goes further back in the tunnel.
No longer able to feel such unbearable pain, she loses Mom now.
She goes away so she can survive, yet Mom was all she had left in life.

Mom needs reaction she use to show well playing out her victim role.
She stops showing her pain within; she becomes safe; the pain is lessening.
Many times as mom hits and screams how she hates her so terribly,
She cries within from far away yet words of hate speak out for her instead.
Family members are angry with her as she's not in her proper reactive role.
She feels nothing it seems to them but hate as she matches mom's screams.

THEN TO TOP HER WHOLE FUCKING LIFE OFF
Mom is even angrier at her for ignoring her "Wonderful Dad."
A Dad she hates with venom within from keeping the burden trapped inside.
When she let him go for the Mom who hates her—she has no one left at all.
And HE HAS THE AUDACITY TO THINK SHE'S BAD!
When she is the one protecting HIS LIE!

After years of trying to survive as she is dying inside,
She finally succeeds and escapes the pain of mom's insanity.
He believes mom now—thinks daughter is mean, bad, cold, and hateful.
As she tells him stories when he gets off of work.

She just began to believe mom is trying to destroy her literally.
Some how by the grace of God a side came out to survive that time.
That if he hadn't buried his head in the sand and chose to ignore,
Such bad, cold, mean, and hateful would have never been born!
Created within an innocent, sensitive child for complete and utter survival.

The innocent, sensitive child buried deep within
Who felt more for everyone in the whole entire family.
To the point she wanted mommy happy and was protecting her Dad.
But all they see is how she is mean and bad.
WHO THE FUCK WAS SEEING AND PROTECTING HER ALL HER LIFE!!!
WHILE SHE WAS BEING HURT ALL THE TIME!!!
HOW DARE SHE HAVE NO FEELINGS AT ALL AS THEY GO ABOUT LIFE IN THEIR ROLES!

When in reality she was the last one with feelings at all!
Just trying to survive the abuse in her life.
He says he didn't know—the man lives a lie.
EVEN WITH HIS VERY OWN SON
RATIONALES TO KEEP HIM FROM BEING THE GUILTY ONE!!!

I have memories and diaries to attest to the many times he stood right by
As she hurt me, screamed, and hit me all the time.
A sister who witnessed the many times
As it took place daily throughout our lives—
RIGHT BEFORE EVERYONE'S EYES.
Not even counting all the many times she was hurting me
When he wasn't there as he went off to work without a care.
To be torn from wanting to tell to protect myself but no words to express.

When in Irvine reality hit—she's literally after my ass!
What's the point of telling the passive woose!
He can't stop her; she's all power; it'll make it worse!
Knowing what a wimp he is all my life the only thing that would happen
She'd get worse but—at least—the hope of a happy family died!

Just try to keep peace for poor dad somewhere inside
While he gives NO FUCK ABOUT YOU AND WHAT YOU GO THROUGH ALL THE TIME!
Later on realizing he must have had a talk with her again
As after he left, I became her victim!

Always trying to get you to fight her telling you she'll kick your ass.
Telling your sister to sit on you as she's bigger than you too.
Pulling your hair, slapping your face, great reflexes run in our family.
Wondering each day what mood she's in and will you be attacked again.

Afraid to call a friend or have someone over
Mom may get mad and blow up all over.
She don't care if you are on the phone or
In the bathtub or in your room.
If you hide, she'll find you.

She told me what a tramp that I was
When I had no boyfriend or slept with no one at all.
She told me how bad and selfish and manipulative too
How sneaky and tricky the real me really was too.
She told me I was all sorts of things I don't even remember.
But I do remember she told me when I got a boyfriend that
Nobody would ever love me once they got to know the real me.

She hurt me over and over again, I began to anticipate with dread.
I can't even take the dog for a walk—everything I did was wrong.
I felt so scared and needed her love, but I was never given it for long.

Towards the end she'd scream how she hated me.
And how she'd live long enough to make me pay
For making her life miserable with Dad again.
How many times did I hear "ARE YOU HAPPY NOW!?"
As dad and her were fighting, and it was my fault.

I'd barely make it through the front door.
She'd be attacking me, and I'd know not what for.
Or I would be in bed and wake up to her tugging me from bed by my hair.
Or she'd hit me with a brush or punch me instead.
Oh, how many times did she pull our hair, slap our face, and rage.
And the punches I never felt but the screaming was constantly hard to bear.

I hated when she said she hated me and that I would amount to nothing.
Even worse when I began to say I hated her back,
And somewhere in the back taking it back.
It killing me that she might believe that.

Near the end I could take no more.
I would just scream on the top of my lungs.
These long shrieking screams that startled her at first as it did me too.
Trying to get her to shut up: Please just leave me alone.
I don't want to fight--I can't take it no more.
Okay, I'm everything that you say.
I'm bad and I'm mean and I'm Queen Shit each day.
Just LEAAAAAAAAAAAAAAAAAAAAAAAAAVE ME ALOOOOOONE!!!
I CAN'T TAKE IT NO MORE!!!!

I'd watch her as she would grow--her face contorted her body blown up.
She would grow and shrink before my eyes, and I would feel nothing inside.
Just wait until she'd go away,
So later she could tell dad what a bad girl I was that day.
I could just listen from the top rail with no voice or words to speak at all.
Or every once in a while, I would just howl down the stairway--
Not wanting him to believe her words but nothing else I could do.
PROTECTING HIM STILL!

She'd scream she hated me so terribly.
I became as loud and ferocious as she.
I startled her a little the first time my screams grew.
Then she threatened Missouri and "the door" as she always taught:
The big, cruel world I'd not survive at all.

The night she kicked me from the house--
Told me she hated me, and I was never allowed back.
I wondered if Dad would come out of his room.
He never did, but I knew that he wouldn't.
He knew better--Mom was all power--Dad a helpless woose.

I tried to run past her to grab clothes for work.
She was hitting and screaming and beating me worse.
I didn't know what I'd done once again.
As I walked in the front door, she bolted from the couch downstairs.
I recognized the monster was out.
She once again screamed AM I HAPPY NOW!!!?
She was on me in a flash, beating me bad, before I knew what hit me again.
Then I knew they had fought about me again.
She chased me up the stairs pulling and yanking and hitting me
As I tried to get away from her grasp.
She tried to get Jenny to sit on me.
She said "Jenny sit on her--you're bigger than her!"
I somewhere inside wondered what mom'd do if Jenny did.
As far as Jenny says she never did as mom said.

I grabbed my pumps and green and black jumpsuit that needed no accessories.
I ran from the house at midnight with her chasing me.
I remember getting in my car and screaming and crying so loud:
I HATE YOU!! I HATE YOU!! I HATE YOU SO BAAAAAAAD!!

I DON'T NEED YOU OR NOBODY EVER AGAIN!!!
I WILL SURVIVE, AND I WILL MAKE IT SOMEDAY!!!
I'LL SHOW YOU—I'LL MAKE IT IN THIS BIG, CRUEL WORLD!!!
I DON'T NEED YOU OR NOBODY EVER!! EVER!! EVER!!
!!!!!!!!!LEEEEEEEEEEEEEAAAAAVVVVVVE MEEEEEEEE ALOOOOOOOOOOOOONE!!!!!!!!!

I drove to my work parking lot.
Slept in my car till 6 o'clock.
I went to work, and my friend said
I could stay the night with her since I had no home left.
The next day her friend said I could stay for a week,
So I could find a home to sleep.
One or two weeks later I moved in with roommates.
I had no idea the peace I would begin to experience.

I began noticing the trees and the flowers and the green grass around me.
I was studying my college homework laying in the yard one day.
I deciphered the feeling was "peace" I was experiencing around me.
I began to call a friend and not worry that I'd be hurt.
I began to socialize and take more classes at school.
They always said "Julie, will never goto college."
They never really knew me—just the scapegoat role they threw on me.

As I was car pooling everyone else around in high school.
Since my life wasn't significant at all.
One day Mom asked with concern if I was happy. I didn't know what that meant.
My friend's mom showed up one day and enrolled me in college—I was afraid.
Then, when I was working full-time and going to school;
Mom screamed I could watch my brother as I'm a freeloader now too.

But it wasn't 'till I moved in with Dan a year later.
When Jenny called me and asked if she could move in with us then.
That was when I began to comprehend, maybe I wasn't so BAD after all.
Jenny said in the phone to me: *Julie, ever since you left mom's after me now!*
Then Dad left Mom after Jenny moved in.
Dad began to make contact with me then. It started out kind of nice.
I noticed since he left her, we could maybe have a relationship.
But it didn't work at all; being around him brought terrible panic inside.
When I wasn't panicking, I felt sooo uncomfortable.
Never having had a Dad, I froze; I didn't know how to be at all.

In Garden Grove, I could take a bath sometimes.
Not worry she'd scream at me or come in and hit me at times.
People don't walk in your bedroom when you close the door.
Unless they knock and you tell them to come in.
I could go about my day, and she wasn't always getting in my way.
But I began hearing her shriek at me in the tub or wherever I was daily.
The familiar sound "!!!JUUUUUUUUUULLLLLLLLLLLIIIIIIIIIIIIIIIEEEEEEEEE!!!!"
I'd tell myself it's okay—I'm in Garden Grove—far from home now.
I kept hearing her scream at me, but I knew I was hearing things.
Not realizing Post Traumatic Stress Disorder was tailing me.

99

The more I grieve, the more I feel.
The more pain and hate resurfaces.
I cry and scream and rage and wail.
My lost life, my childhood.

I gather through Jenny's letter this time distant, typed, and not signed.
She pry had a talk with Dad some how again.
Whenever he's in the picture our relationship starts lacking too.
Some how as usual he doesn't even have to try.
The roles in our family for so long molded in time.
She can't help herself, she feels nothing at all!
I guess she's been talking to good old illusional Dad.
Who cares only to save his VERY OWN HIDE!
THAT FUCKING BASTARD SOME HOW ALWAYS RUINING LIVES!
LIKE IN THERAPY A BLACK SWIRLING TORNADO
WITH HIS FACE AT THE HEAD WHEN DISCUSSING SABOTAGE.
How many other times after contact by him in my life.
At work, in relationships--too many times.

He spends his life walking around concerned with only his image.
Not caring about my life--NOT FROM THE BEGINNING!
JUST THROWS OUT JUDGMENTS AT THE SO-CALLED "LOSERS" OF THIS WORLD.
His threats, ultimatums, manipulations, and guilt.
Control at any price with emotions well contained.
Smiles on the outside to live up to his image.
Control deep within to contain all his emotions.
Until much later some kind of contorted,
Emotional, blown-up explosion of words.
When can't get me to conform to his ways.
I'm learning self-love and boundaries today.

He tells me "At least I have one loyal daughter."
As long as she does what he says or shame is triggered.
She always knew how to get by with political talk he taught and likes.
His love will never be more important than my value to myself.
I now know the truth of the sensitive, loving child who resides within.
She gave her life away to try and save a family.
While the other "loyal" daughter could give a flying fuck!
Who never tried to save a family but hid in her bedroom a lot.
That is the daughter who you consider SO LOYAL.
Well, you two have a good life together!

I FINALLY KNOW WHO THE LOVING ONE IS IN THIS FAMILY.
SHE IS NOT THE ONE YOU HAVE A RELATIONSHIP WITH AS SHE IS HEALING.
HEALING FROM A LIFETIME OF SENSITIVITY--ABUSE DROVE HER TO ESCAPE REALITY.
THE ONE WHO NEVER HAD TO COPE WITH ALL THE SHIT I WENT THROUGH.
CAN HAVE A JOB, A HUSBAND, KIDS, A FATHER TOO.
!!!!!!!!!!!!!! IT'S COMPLETE BULLSHIT, YET THE TRUTH !!!!!!!!!!!!!!!!!!!!!!

Tammy says there is never ONE sick in the family.
Each has a role to play; yet, some roles are more favorable.
Other roles make you seek help right away.
I stopped playing--I got out!
The victim's gone. I respect myself now.
I will be scapegoat for no one ever again.

Not to put my sister down as she had her share of abuse to go around.
She is still in denial about her childhood life, and maybe she can get by.
Maybe for whatever reason she has processed it all and is alright.
But obviously her inability to feel at times--
A result of abuse she has not healed inside.
Maybe the pain hasn't reached the point where seeking help is desirable.

She can think how great that he is.
She can even believe it for as long as she lives.
BUT SHE WILL NEVER TELL ME MY ANGER IS NOT JUSTIFIED.
I AM VALIDATED TIME AFTER TIME.
Unbelievable his bullshit words are today.
How dare I speak in this tone about "loving Dad."
Well, Dad, if you had access to care,
You would never have tolerated the abuse as you did.
You may right me off as a "psycho."
The difference is I know better today.
It doesn't matter no more what you think.
I'm healing, I'm good, and you can not make me hate.
I will no longer sabotage my life because of you.
Who taught me my value when I had no clue.
If you ever read this you may hate me for speaking the truth.
I doubt you could ever hear and face in you the God, awful truth!

As I recovered as an adult and anger began to show up.
HE HAD THE AUDACITY TO BE ANGRY AT ME FOR MY FEELINGS!!!!
AS MY FEELINGS FROZEN FINALLY COME OUT
SO I CAN MAYBE HAVE A CHANCE TO LIVE!!--HOW DARE ME AGAIN!!!
ANGRY AT ME FOR ALL MY AMBIVALENT FEELINGS ONE DAY FROZEN AWAY,
AND IN RECOVERY BEGINNING TO COME OUT AND SPEAK TODAY.
ONE DAY TELLING ME HOW PROUD OF MY PROGRAM HE IS
UNTIL MY PROGRAM TEACHES ME BOUNDARIES WITH HIM.
MY FEELINGS MAKE HIM HAVE TO LOOK AT HIMSELF A LITTLE BIT!
HE DID NOT WANT TO HEAR ANYTHING THAT MAY MAKE HIM HURT.
IT JUST MAY INCONVENIENCE HIS DAY OR HIS SCHEDULE A BIT!
WHEN I LOST ALL CAPACITY TO FEEL FOR MANY YEARS YOU SON OF A BITCH!
I'M NO LONGER CONCERNED IF YOU FEEL SHITTY FOR ONE FUCKING WEEK!
I'M NOT WORRYING IF MY WORDS COME OUT ANGRY,
EXPLOSIVE, OR MEAN, IT'S ABOUT TIME YOU LISTEN TO ME!!!!!!!

He's the one who let me go when feelings turned off so long ago.
When I was just a little girl WHO NEEDED A PROTECTIVE FATHER, you know.
I knew I'd be a toss away easily to him.
Just throw me away--He already had.

What if I don't do as he says? I don't know, but I do know.
I don't care. It's too late.
He only truly accepts those who mold to his liking.
That is not acceptable to me ever again.
I am me, and I am good exactly as I am.

TO HAVE A RELATIONSHIP WITH ME IF I EVER SO DESIRED,
HE'D HAVE TO ACTUALLY HEAR ANGER AND RAGE--FEELINGS NOT IN HIS VOCABULARY!
HE WOULD HAVE TO LOOK AT HIMSELF FOR ONCE IN HIS LIFE--
INSTEAD OF POINTING FINGERS AT MOM OR SOMEONE ELSE OUTSIDE.
LOOK AT HIMSELF WITH ALL HIS BURIED PAIN.
I DON'T THINK EVEN A POSSIBILITY FOR HIM.
EVEN IF HE COULD HANDLE ACKNOWLEDGING HIS PART,
MY BROTHER AND HIS NEGLECT OF HIM FOR YEARS HAS BEEN UNACCEPTABLE!

All the years he let me down with my bro; I was all alone.
I needed support; I had no where to turn.
Even my sister when I was near the end.
She hangs up on me when I needed her help with our bro.
I never ask her for anything.
I felt something die inside of me.
I lost a father, then a mother, and then my sister in the end.
But the good news is I'm healing after all these years.

As far as Dad, I have no idea, as I'm still processing rage everyday.
But Jenny, my sister, we share a special bond.
There may be a chance we can build a relationship some how.
The only way I'm willing to have a relationship with her again
Is if we can feel our true feelings
Without the influence of other family members.
I have a therapist who by the grace of God I'm healing.
The people I choose to be around in my life are people who FEEL inside.
I never had a dad, and my mother who I love is dead.
My brother is the only one left, and we have a relationship.
As far as my sister, it's up to her now.
How important our relationship is as I'm not trying no more.

I think many times as I heal in therapy,
It would be actually easier to stay away from my family.
Since I'm not around them my life flows more easily.
Some how even hearing his voice brings out sabotage really bad in me!
So many years of abuse & insanity-a family in denial of what it's done to me.
My ex-husband taught me the only unconditional love I grew to know,
And for that I will always be grateful.
I had a husband who knew more about my brother's life
Than his own father or sister who asked me questions all the time.
Bobby just like his sister learned early enough
Who you can't count on to be there where it really counts.

I wonder will I ever want a relationship with you?
A father I lost so long ago that it's taken a lifetime to heal?

Grieving the loss of a father and letting him go.
Especially when I know so well he's so inflexible.
Doesn't he even say himself: People don't change much at all.
He tries to change others or find those who mold to his like.
Once I'm whole, I can forgive him and move on with my life.
It doesn't have to be good or bad, just wish him the best.
What exactly do we have left to establish now?
We neither know how to be with each other at all.

Even Jenny said it herself in her letter to me.
"He is really 'happy with her'" his wife to be.
His love is never unconditional and that is not acceptable to me.
I know my value now after years of recovery, healing, and therapy.
And all the years he let me down with his very own son.
After Mom died and Bobby had no one.
He's no different with his son today
Than his daughter who needed him as a little girl.
He can use whichever rationale lets his mind off the hook.
The bottomline is that when you love someone YOU'RE THERE NO MATTER WHAT.

BOBBY IS NOT AN OPTION AS THE FAMILY SEEMS TO THINK!
A family not capable of emotional support.
The true brainwasher I am beginning to see as I heal—
Is the father who taught the family feelings were crazy to feel!
The only emotional support ever given to me bizarre as it may be
Was by the mom who when feeling went berserk from unhealed pain!
Her pain was made much worse—as well—from her marrying the wrong person.
A man incapable of experiencing unpleasant feelings at all.
Taught to keep his feelings under control from his own life of repression.

And for Grandma who everyone thinks is so great!
Ask her why she would tell her granddaughter to piss on the street!
Ask her why she would tell her granddaughter to jump in the trunk!
Ask her why she wouldn't take her to a restroom when she had to go!
Ask her why she would try and shame her granddaughter at all!
Looking back on that day, I noticed my not reacting was making her hate.
I didn't assume my victim role—I communicated calmly to her.
Then it all makes sense; mother—like son—it fits!
They do not know how to respond to healthy assertiveness at all.
Dad needed Mom and all her emotions as anger in him is frozen.
If mom had not become reactive, Dad would have felt his anger.

That's why years later Dad freaked out at me.
It was because I remained so calm as he screamed.
How does it feel, Dad, to know what it's like to love someone
WHEN THEY DON'T CARE OR KEEP FEELINGS HIDDEN INSIDE?
See, Dad, I had a perfect role model through you.
You taught me as a child who NOT TO FEEL CLOSE TO.
I know my emotions will NOT BE HEARD with you.
So why goto that place and open my heart where it will only be hurt by you?

IT MAKES YOU FEEL KIND OF CRAZY, DOESN'T IT, DAD?
TO NEED A REACTION *OR AT LEAST TO BE HEARD AT ALL*
BUT THAT DIDN'T *MAKE* YOU CRAZY DID IT, DAD?
!!THAT MAKES YOU A NORMAL, FEELING HUMAN BEING WHO IS HURT AND MAD!!
YOU NEGLECTED MOM LEFT AND RIGHT KNOWING SHE NEEDED YOUR EMOTIONAL SUPPORT.
THE MORE YOU NEGLECTED HER NEEDS, SHE SCREAMED (LIKE YOU DID WITH ME),
!!!AND YOU TRIED TO CONVINCE HER SHE'S CRAZY!!!

She wouldn't have behaved so emotionally unstably
If you had been there and heard her originally.
Like years later you wished from me
As you freaked out while I told you to calm down basically.
Repeating words you taught when so very young:
"No one can make you *feel anything* unless you consent."
Isn't that one of the many things you always said?
Now you know the truth, Dad, and it doesn't have to make you "crazy."
When you care about another and they do not hear you at all,
It's like talking to a wall—and that can MAKE ANYONE QUITE VOLATILE!
Unless they go around after a while feeling nothing at all.
Yet if you think about it: The ones still becoming volatile
In an atmosphere that it is not safe to feel at all.
At least they are the ONLY ONES FEELING AT ALL.
Desiring human connection as FEELING brings EMOTIONS to ALL.
It comes down to the real question:
Who is safe and will play fair with your emotions
Once you become whole and have access to them all?

As far as Grandma, now in therapy, I'm putting it together.
It may have something to do with my telling her about a flashback.
Having know idea at the time what it meant,
Yet she knew very well and must have thought I knew something.
She began treating me degradingly ever since as her guilt was blossoming.
If she has nothing to hide, TELL ME THE TRUTH ABOUT THAT ROOM.
BECAUSE WHETHER OR NOT YOU DO, I AM REMEMBERING.
I KNOW THAT DAD'S BROTHER KNOWS TOO, AND DAD I'M NOT SURE OF—TOO SOON.
YET IF HE DOES, IT WOULD EXPLAIN EVEN MORE
WHY I'VE HATED HIM ALL THESE YEARS.
Whatever happened, the truth is coming out.
So you might as well tell me now.
I experienced something that made me split inside
And sends me into black terror everytime.

Maybe they figured it's better off buried.
She was barely a little girl; let's forget it ever happened.
It's better that way; she'll never remember; kid's are so resilient.
It will not affect her life; it's over and done with now.
It has lived frozen inside me alive each day.
Affecting my perceptions in every way.
The truth is it has destroyed my life.
I need to remember, so I can heal it and process it and let it go.

You might just try something, Jen.
Talk to her person to person separately from Dad.
Tell her Julie's getting a memory of her bedroom in downtown L.A.
She's there and H_____, her other son, and just watch her face.
Not only watch her face then; but give her a week to digest it.
If it's no big deal, she can tell us all what happened.
Ask her why she was telling her to "Be Quiet, Julie."
A flashback to her downtown L.A. bedroom with lots of people there.
That sends me straight into black terror!

Ask her why she talked so condescendingly to me on the cruise,
And when I stayed for a week after leaving Steve.
She treats me so dehumanizing and disrespects Mom who is dead saying:
"You're crazy just like she was" when I turned around and said:
"EXCUSE ME," and she changed her choice of words.
When all I did was respect her rule to not let anyone know I was there.
I heard a knock on the door but couldn't look through the peekhole.
She had it blocked off. If I opened the door, they'd know she had a guest.
Later I found out it was her, and she told me I did it on purpose.
Why would I ever do that kind of insanity?!
Except that it's like dejavu of her in my past reality.
I was in tears as I told her I didn't even leave to *eat* till she got back.
Because I wanted to *make sure* she wouldn't be locked out!
I never understood why she didn't just say "Julie, it's me."
So I'd know and open the door accordingly.

When I try to write her behavior off as "senility,"
I begin to notice she doesn't treat me badly when others are around.
Just when we are alone so she has control of herself!
Ask her why she tries to make me feel bad
After I left Steve and was just trying to hold on.
I was looking for a home, a job, and healing from a broken heart.
It's like childhood again--you're vulnerable and they hurt you more.
She even accused me of taking her shit I wouldn't want in the first place!
I'm not protecting her bullshit no more either.
There's some weird shit in our family, and IT'S NOT MY FAULT!

Just because someone has been hurt in the past,
And just because they are vulnerable and dependent.
That is how you know who truly cares for you.
Because the ones *who do, do not* use it against you.
Just because mom needed you, Dad.
That doesn't mean you manipulate her to get what you want.
Just because she was abused and raised in an orphanage, Grandma.
Doesn't mean she is worth less and deserves that treatment repeated by you!
She is coming out too many years later to count.
She knows her family is not a safe place to be vulnerable around!
What is the point being around them at all?
When that's never been a safe atmosphere to relax and be herself?

If Jen and I want a relationship someday,
She'll need to be honest as we communicate.
Let out any hostility she may still feel,
Possibly in a therapy session or two.
So, we can start anew relating as sisters and friends too.
I want her to love me and not indirectly shine me with letters unsigned.
Or other methods of passive aggression she may try and hide.

You may consider a suggestion, Jen.
No matter if it's directly, indirectly, or in gest.
Dad has had a great impact on our lives—and how we feel inside.
So if you wish to continue writing sometime.
You may wish to have boundaries with him about our life.
You may think you are strong and will not be influenced by his words.
However, I've experienced in my own life it doesn't work.
If you truly want our relationship to grow,
You will need to keep our relationship separate from your life with him.
Tell him to be quiet if he shoots at the mouth.
He always talks of respect. Respect to him is honor without a voice.
Not that I hate him though a few inside at this point in recovery do.
The way I feel about Dad goes from love to hate fluctuating rapidly still.
Hate is actually closer to love than years of feeling nothing at all.
Now I get to feel every single feeling inside.
And know it's alright—I'm entitled to mine.

If you wish to continue to communicate with me,
Notice how you feel after being around him.
If that affects how you feel about me at this time,
Like around my wedding when he began telling you his side.
You may wish to tell him to talk to his mom instead,
As you and I grow stronger and learn who we are not influenced by him.
Like you said a long time ago before you had Jay.
"We're all we got," and I love you still today.
Our relationship is not about you, me, and dad.
It's about us getting to know each other again if we still both want that.
We need to be who we are without our designated family role.
To confuse the boundaries and make us uncomfortable.
As for Dad, I don't desire him back right now.
I have much healing left to do and that's what I'm focusing on.

I'm beginning to develop itsy, bitsy relationships.
Although they usually don't last or go away still.
No one is THAT SAFE for me yet.
I'm still building safety within that was never given as a kid.
As soon as I care, the system protects us still.
Two little examples of this below:
I was eating with friends who asked me something after a volleyball game.
The more often I saw them, it began triggering the system.
I heard somewhere inside a voice saying to me:
You want to get close—don't pull away.

I shared my heart a little that day instead of switching and becomimg mean.
But then never went back afterward, it was too scary.

A couple days ago, I wanted to wash a pan that was dirty as a favor.
No big deal—I knew it was my roommate's who had recently helped me.
He drove me to pick up my car the other day.
It was just a nice gesture I wanted to display.
Then I became terrified and realized I was afraid.
What if he walked in and caught me washing his pan?
Then I deciphered I was afraid of being attacked.

I battled within, Why would he hurt me—I'm just being nice?
I realized 'cause that's when Mom attacked me all the time.
I was just trying to love her, and the more that I did,
She hurt me over and over again.
It wasn't for things that I did that were bad.
It was for loving her and being vulnerable—a sweet, innocent child.

So I finished everything in the kitchen I needed to do—
Then I washed the pan and left real soon.
So far it has not triggered my system with him which can make enemies quick.
That's why I've learned to be careful everywhere I go to not care or feel.
Especially the more important or necessary that person or home may be.
As soon as I do, the patterns and insanity.
Because I need peace and a home to sleep,
I stay in my room so no feelings are triggered that could jeopardize me,
As I get help and build internal safety.

I'm learning little by little to change my behavior.
As the little ones' heal and can stay still longer.
Little by little we decipher no one's hurting us any longer.
I've been terrified most my life yet my biggest asset
Is my greatest weakness: The system's strength inside.
All the protectors kept me alive.
While the wounded ones remain hidden most the time.

People have been impossible ALL my life.
Temporary moments of people I cared with is all I remember:
A father who I lost when I was way too young it's hardly a memory.
A Mom who broke my heart more times than I can count.
A brother whose innocence was safe to be around.
A sister who would rather be with friends than ever hang with me.

Crystal back in second grade—Lynn Carney in seventh.
A short time with Debbie in college.
You as a little child, when we moved to Irvine, and before you met Jay.
Dan who was as dysfunctional as I—
Yet his unconditional love taught me value inside.
Shanda who moved far away who was real and authentic.
A papa after I left Dan who helped me see my sides.
My soulmate who I recently left as I thought I'd die.

They were the ones who touched my heart.
I have never been able to maintain "healthy" in my life.
I've lived a pretty solitary life.
Yet to a people person inside that's a tremendous loss.
People are what makes life living at all.

Unable to develop relationships or closeness
Without terror and switching and pain for years.
Now FINALLY SOME 20+ YEARS LATER, I'M BEGINNING TO FEEL AGAIN.
LEARN TO LIVE AGAIN YET I FEEL QUITE FRAGILE AND SCARED MOST THE TIME.
THE ONLY PEOPLE I HAVE IN MY LIFE ARE OTHER SURVIVORS
WHO I TRUST INSIDE OVER TIME.
I AM BUILDING SAFETY WITHIN TO TRUST COMING OUT MORE OFTEN.

I will not judge your relationship with Dad.
But I will tell you this, Jen.
I DO REMEMBER HE WAS THERE OVER AND OVER
MANY, MANY TIMES AND STOOD RIGHT BY
WHILE MOM ATTACKED ME, HIT ME, and SCREAMED ALL THE TIME.
SO WERE YOU, JEN, MORE TIMES THAN YOU REMEMBER.
I DON'T BLAME YOU AS YOU WERE JUST A LITTLE GIRL TOO.
BUT HE WAS OUR DAD AND HE SHOULD'VE DONE SOMETHING—ANYTHING AT ALL!
I LOST MY LIFE AS A RESULT OF HIS NO ACTIONS.
But even all that I could let go of as some how his pitiful role.

But what for a lifetime has made me BOIL INSIDE
Is my LOVE AND LOYALTY TO THE BASTARD ALL MY FUCKING LIFE!
Trying to save him from Mom's raging wrath as I DIE.
Having no clue I'M A CHILD—
He's SUPPOSE TO BE THE RESPONSIBLE ADULT IN OUR LIFE!
ALL THAT I LOST TO SURVIVE,
WHICH WASN'T A DESIRE OR OPTION *IT JUST HAPPENED INSIDE.*
SURVIVAL TOOK OVER AS THAT'S HOW BAD WAS MY REAL LIFE!

THEN I LIVE THE REST OF MY LIFE WITH HIM TIP TOEING AROUND PANIC INSIDE
AS ALL THE LITTLE ONES ARE HIDING, TERRIFIED, AND CRYING INSIDE.
KNOWING TOO WELL THE REALITY OF DAD AROUND HUMAN EMOTIONS ALIVE.
REPRESSING MY ANGRY SIDES THAT IN ORDER FOR ME TO HEAL MUST COME ALIVE.
!!!SO DAD WON'T BE MAD AT ME *FOR MY FEELINGS* AS THEY BURST FROM INSIDE!!!
AS I BOIL AND BOIL AND BOIL INSIDE TRYING TO MAINTAIN THEM
AND CONTROL THEM AS HE LIKES. PRAYING EACH TIME HE COMES TO THE DOOR,
I CAN MAINTAIN AND REMAIN CALM SOME HOW YET KNOWING IT'S BECOMING USELESS!!
!!!!THEY ARE COMING OUT, AND I CAN'T STOP THEM NO MORE!!!!
AND WHY WOULD I EVER WANT TO IN THE FIRST PLACE?
EXCEPT THAT I GUESS SOMEWHERE INSIDE *WE CARE* WHAT HE FEELS AND THINKS!!!!
TERRIFIED OF LOSING A DAD WE ALREADY LOST AND HAD NEEDED ALL OUR LIFE.
SO HE CAN CALL ME A "GRADE-A FUCKING BITCH" AND BLOW ME TO THE SIDE.
!!!!!!!!!!NO UNCONDITIONAL LOVE EVER IN MY LIFE!!!!!!!!!!

HAVING HIM DO JUST LIKE HE DID ALL MY CHILDHOOD!!!
!!!!BLOW OFF MY FEELINGS LIKE I MATTER NOT FUCKING AT ALL!!!!
NOT NO MORE AS I HAVE A VOICE NOW AND *I AM* SO VERY LOVABLE AND VALUABLE.
Through an ex-husband and God,
I have learned how it feels to be unconditionally valued and loved.

Whatever you decide, I wish you a good life.
I truly am beginning to feel *good* after all this time.
No exteriors necessary in my life.
Layers peeling away—I am healing each day.
Living is becoming possible for me today.
If you wish not to write at this time,
Possibly in a few years we could talk sometime.
I wish you, Jay, Natalie, and Nathan the best in life.

HELL

Impenetrable fear and darkness;
Driven to death as exit out.
Enthralled in death's grasp--flash of eternal hell;
Awareness *NO ESCAPE* at all.

In utter terror I needed life;
God bring me back to the light far from agony inside.
Fleeting visit of hell's fury--*NO WAY OUT*--I must stay.
My soul is not free so eternal pain.

Despair and desolation I had come to know.
Years of fantasy escape brought temporary hope.
Instant truth struck so complete when death upon me:
DOOM NEVER-ENDING.

Insanity I could not bear everlasting;
No way to endure life yet death no option either.
I must find God so I can bear the pain each day;
This blink of life I've come to hate.

Fill my spirit with your love;
So I can bear this suffering and carry on.
Trust your strength to get me through;
Some day I may rest in peace with you.

GOD'S LOVE

Unconditionally loved, valued, and forgiven each day.

Heart glowing with God's love; you are blessed and radiate.

Living like Christ becomes a hunger too;

Your truth and God's combine and become one in you.

You live each moment of life with passion; you are free to be as God desires.

Jesus is God in human form with humanness, imperfections, and all.

There is hope since we've been given grace.

We can become like His Son--it's never too late.

Once confessed, you can access your true spirit.

You accept self so no need to judge others either.

No need to hate when nobody to defend.

It becomes clear--I'M LOVED, VALUED, AND FORGIVEN!

If everyone followed their truth with courage and integrity,

God's message would be heard through each of us--don't you see?

Happiness is being exactly who you are

As an already forgiven child of God.

ANXIETY ATTACK

Internal conflict within;
Which side's view is important?

Who to be, how to be,
What to be, which side of me?

Chaos, frustration, panic disorder;
Performance to impress the world.

When did who I am matter?
To love myself and calm the chatter.

So much terror and shame;
I'm so tired of caring what you think.

Just be me whoever I am;
So my insides match my outsides, and I calm down.

Wouldn't it be nice if God's love was felt by all,
And we could be ourselves wherever we are?

WEIGHED DOWN BY DEPRESSION

Emotions held inside;
No longer claimed as mine.

Don't even know they're gone;
Misery for so long.

Never let them out;
Pain inescapable still.

Wonder why it's dark;
Feeling is impossible.

They tell you to take a pill;
The problem is chemical.

No prescription will set me free;
I must let each side speak.

When we let our feelings flow;
Joy and peace will be known.

CO-DEPENDENCY CURE

No need to control;
I am lovable.
No need to perform;
God loves me as I am.
No need to cling;
I matter within.
No need to play games;
I am filled with integrity.
No need to please;
Acceptance is inside of me.
No need to fear you'll leave;
God takes care of me.
I may love you openly;
No longer fear you may hurt me, betray me, or stray.
I can love you without hate;
I feel your wounds and know you're in pain.
When my soulmate and I connect;
We won't have to try—it'll be permanent.
Everyone else on this journey we meet;
Spread love and hope to brighten their day.

LIFE
COMPARTMENTALIZED

Emotions frozen and disowned;

Living separate lives of their own.

How do you get to the other side;

Vision limited by whose eyes.

I wanna feel like seconds before,

But know that, that's impossible.

I've long since learned no control of the switch;

The good news is she'll come back again.

When I feel like Sally or Joe,

Hope I don't blink wrong.

If I do, it's too late;

Their feelings just go away.

Try and remember when Sam is out

That living is some how possible.

Each side eventually goes away;

Nothing to do but wait.

After years you'd think I'd comprehend;

Yet each side's life feels real again.

It's so difficult to remember each time;

Don't act on my feelings as they're not mine.

And when Cindy's love is out;

There is surely a papa around.

But with her love and childish need;

Comes such unbearable pain.

When she loves, nothing else matters;

Then, Sandy takes over, and no more papa.

Besides even if Cindy could stay,

Functioning becomes harder each day.

Veronica tries to be kind to someone;

Terror takes over for feeling at all.

Ju Ju comes out and we're gone for a time;

Or Vicky takes over--no more terror--people gone from our life.

If Vicky don't come out with her rage and all,

Margaret runs and hides with fear and shame inside.

Vicky makes others go away,

And Margaret can't face each day.

Sabotage makes us always late
With strange coincidences all over the place.
Rose monitors us all or closes the door;
Veronica trying so hard to maintain control.

Veronica's awesome strength
Trying desperately to make our life okay.
Yet she's running in place;
She has no control of us each day.

JWK's love bringing us peace;
Yet reminder she's a side too and can't stay.
So back to therapy twice a week
To put us back together so we can integrate.

LIVING IN THE PRESENT

The more the pain is out of me;
Terror, despair, and desperate need.
All the trapped ones inside come out;
We are still alive somehow!

Darkness begins to fade away;
We become so grateful when we awake.
Doom is going; we matter again.
People we pass seem more like friends.

As it becomes bearable to feel,
Life becomes a miracle.
For so long we've lived in misery,
Frozen in childhood memories.

Now more often we see light
And know we are beginning life.
We begin experiencing each day
Lost feelings of me from yesterday.

Cups runneth over are emptying,
And we are living our present feelings.
What a way to live each day--
Let the little ones out all over the place.

Then we are free to be
Presently feeling and being me.

CYCLE BACK
TO LOVE

HURT BREEDS HATE.
HATE MAY LEAD TO PERPETRATION.
PERPETRATION INSTILLS SHAME.
SHAME CAUSES DESOLATION.
DESOLATION MOVES TOWARD ALIENATION.
ALIENATION SPREADS INDIFFERENCE.
INDIFFERENCE BREEDS GLIMPSES OF HATE.
HATE REVEALS UNRESOLVED PAIN AND
SO THE CYCLE GOES. . . .

GOD GIVES LOVE.
GOD'S LOVE TEACHES VALUE.
VALUE SPREADS FORGIVENESS.
FORGIVENESS MELTS HATE.
HATE DISSOLVED GIVES BACK LOVE.
UNCONDITIONAL LOVE BRINGS HEALING.
HEALING BRINGS BACK LIFE.
BEING SAVED ENCOURAGES SERVING HIM.
SERVITUDE CREATES MORE LOVE AND
SO THE CYCLE GOES. . . .

REFLECTING
CHRIST

Whatever feeling inside of you that you've disowned or separated from is unresolved. So, everywhere you go you see it in everyone else because it's unresolved in you. Once it is resolved in you, you'll stop seeing it in others and only see the purity state--the truth of another human soul--because you will be reflecting your own truth back to you as all your emotions will be free--no longer disowned or forgotten. You will know and see your true loving, pure state. In knowing this, when you look at others, you will see their own.

There will be no judgment of others because you will no longer judge yourself because you will be whole and free internally living in that eternal bliss--God's love. We are all mirrors looking outward thinking we are looking at someone. Yet, we are truly looking in a mirror that reflects our inner self. What we are truly seeing in others is a mirror reflection of what in us we haven't become free or resolved of yet. So, the best thing to do when someone else really upsets us or a particular trait, attitude, emotion, behavior, or personality really tee's us off is to just ask yourself *What in myself hasn't been resolved?* Then, pray and wait. It will surface, and then you can process it and be free of it. You'll know when you're healed when everywhere you go and everyone you meet you see reflected back to you love and peace because since you are reflecting your own mirror's reflection--the eyes into your soul--then if you're seeing love and peace and bliss everywhere that means your own spirit is free.

Then, you finally know the truth--God's truth--with the sacrifice of Christ. There is no guilt--no judgment--we've already been forgiven and each day we start fresh letting go of the past so that we may stay in the eternal bliss of a free, loving spirit. And because we know God's love for us and now love ourself, we can spread that love everywhere we go without reacting to someone else's pain as a result of our own unresolved pain. Instead, let them be, with love, understanding their wounds and their journey process is their own. Our love for them in the midst of their journey may be the catalyst to their own internal truth that even with all human sin and unresolved pain, they are still inherently loved.

That truth reflecting through you may just cause them to break down in relief and cry and let all their own walls of ego and pride and pain dissipate as they reach the truth too. Or, at least, you may have softened a spot on their possibly hardened, bitter heart that may help them in their own journey process to freedom.

No wonder in the Lord's prayer it says "Thy will be done on earth as it is in heaven" because in heaven there is eternal bliss. God loves us so much that he would like us to experience that bliss here on earth and heal the world through His will. His will, will bring that bliss and peace of heaven. The only reason it's not present on earth is that in heaven we see the truth of our oneness. We know the truth, so the peace and bliss are present.

Here on earth we forget--through fear and ego and perceived separate selves via our separate bodies and our layers of buried pain that we walk around transferring and projecting onto others. We are all like ping pong balls bouncing off each other all over the place unless we are lucky enough to see the truth through God's word and God's presence. Unfortunately, as human beings who were given free will, motivation may only come through much earthly pain.

But once God's presence clears the clouds to the truth, we are healed of our internal struggles and can let it all go and surrender completely and trust in the process and accept things exactly as they are. We will know that nothing of this world matters, and our spirits will continue on in eternal bliss. We may learn this lesson now and thus experience great pleasure here on earth or learn it in the hereafter for those on the pathway to eternal bliss.

I remember in 1997 my own clouds began to part. Then, the love set me free for a time, and I was no longer in fear even over a job and how long it lasted. It didn't matter if I had one job for 50 years or 50 jobs in one year. My purpose was not my work--my job--and my value was not reliant upon anything I do. I am inherently valuable just because I exist. My purpose was to love those I come in contact with throughout my day--no matter where I am. Life is a process and love is the purpose and everything else is just not important except for the purpose of spreading love and healing to this earthly world. As in the end, all of this world will perish yet the love will live in us forever.

As I help spread love--or at least not project my own pain to others--and as I allow feelings to surface as they do, I feel free. Freedom to be me at every given moment. I may exude kindness to others and help others however I can. Maybe it's in how I do things or how I succeed in life. Maybe it's sharing my experience and how I feel. I may share with others yet, at moments, the fear rises again. My reflex action is to hold back love out of fear. My fear is that if I share or feel or whatever else, there will be less for me or I'll have more competition some how. Then I keep sharing anyway as (1) I remember those who helped me along the way'; (2) I remember with pure love there is no fear; (3) I remember that love is infinite; and (4) I remember the point is to love.

The only thing that will bring bad things my way is the holding back of love, which is then fear. And whatever you live your life in is what is reflected back to you. I choose to live in love today as my experience has proven that to the extent I am in "love" and sharing that "love" with others to that same extent I am free and alive and happy and at peace. And for no other reason, I want to feel that on earth as this blink of time here on earth feels like one mighty long blink. So if I am here a while, I would like to enjoy this time. As God brings me healing, I am grateful and want to share His joy with others to serve Him for saving me.

I got a glimpse into understanding in the Bible what may have been what frightened me so by the Book of David when God placed an evil spirit in Saul and then Saul reacting to that evil spirit exhibited evil behavior and, thus, lived a miserable life and ended up sacrificing his own life. It's like Saul was not following God's will in the first place--not walking the path of righteousness. If we all are mirrors, and we inherently know the truth deep within underneath all our layers of pain--and yet we do behavior against this truth--that sin we can't hide from ourself or the holy spirit within us.

So we become how we see ourself which from our sinful nature only gets progressively worse. Thus, we sin further in defeat which contradicts our true nature. Therefore, we live a miserable existence and die from our own judgment of that truth. Yet, if we let him, God through the holy spirit will heal us of our evil spirit. All we need to do is be willing--with our free will--to obey Him by repenting. He does not require we live a sinless life following the laws of this world perfectly as he knows our natures as humans is to sin--he created us--and we would fail miserably.

But, instead, He only asks that we have faith in Him through Jesus Christ our savior (whose death and resurrection bring us forgiveness of our sins) and repent of our sins and ask forgiveness through the holy spirit. In doing just that every time we sin, we are continually cleansed back to our true state of purity so that the holy spirit within us shines through.

Then, we no longer desire a sinful life. And the laws of the world that we would typically want to defy and disobey--as a result of rebellious hearts--are unimportant. The only law we follow now is the law of God which more and more resides within us through Christ and creates in us the kind of people in this world God would desire of us.

We can become more like the image of Christ and stay this way more often because we don't have so many layers of self-hate building on each other in us that make us judge ourselves. That judgment and guilt and shame cause us to hide from ourself the feared truth of our self-worth. Yet that very hiding from ourself and others perpetuates our cycle of self-hate and mirrored reflection, which then attempts to spread itself outward to others for fear of catching a glimpse ourself.

And others may *catch* some of our projection from belief in their own unworthiness not yet resolved. Yet God has said from the beginning that He has saved the world. Those who believe in Him shall have eternal life. We have been forgiven of our sins. If we place our eyes and ears on Him, we will know the truth.

Yet some of us still struggle because we fear if God knew the truth of our sinful nature, He'd strike us down. That is because we already know the truth of our sinful nature and have been projecting it outward thinking we should be struck down. Yet all he wants us to do is give it to Him, and we are forgiven. And in this very forgiveness comes the freedom. A clean slate to start anew each day. Because without that grace we would have given up on ourself.

We would have assumed: *I have messed up way too badly so I give up on me and become all that evil that I believe I am and deserve.* Although all those layers are only covering the truth of our innocence and beauty that we forgot when born to this earthly world where we became human sinners rebelling the laws of the world. Yet, God already knows this as He created us and through Christ we have been saved--forgiven.

So we can become our heavenly spirit again on earth as in heaven. And because our slate is cleaned often by repenting and through forgiveness and grace, we are closer to the holy spirit within us. The layers internally are not built so high each time as we learn this truth. So we can become our true spirit's desire as the mirror is clear and our reflection is closer to the image of Christ that lives within us, and this brings glory to God.

CONTACT AND PURCHASE/ORDER

Author welcomes your personal story. You may contact the author, and this book may be purchased and personally signed by the author by sending a check or money order for $20.00 (per copy) made payable to Julie Martin at the address referenced below. This price includes shipping and handling costs. Please be sure to include your current mailing address and allow two weeks delivery time. This book will soon be made available for e-publishing through author's website and other sites on-line. Author has a PayPal account. Author has done book readings and author signings at Barnes & Noble and will be conducting workshops soon. Her book has been exhibited in child abuse conferences throughout the United States.

Julie Martin
Julie Martin's Miracle System, a
division of MIRACLE SYSTEM PRESS
P.O. Box 3852
Costa Mesa, CA 92628-3852
www.jmmiraclesystempress.com
writejuliem@jmmiraclesystempress.com

Distributors/Wholesalers:

Baker & Taylor, P.O. Box 6885, Bridgewater, NJ 08807-0885, 908/541-7436, 800/775-1500, (ph), www.btol.com, jacobsj@btol.com (Jonathan Jacobson, Buyer).

Brodart, Co., 500 Arch Street, Williamsport, PA 17701, 570/326-2461, 800/233-8467 x6511, (ph), www.brodart.com, mason@brodart.com (Donna Wagner, Buyer).

Dustbooks, P.O. Box 100, Paradise, CA 95967, 800/477-6110, 530/877-6110 (ph), 530/877-0222 (fax), www.dustbooks.com, dustbooks@dcsi.net.

Emery-Pratt Company, 1966 West Main Street, Owosso, MI 48867-1397, 800/248-3887, 517/723-5291 (p), 800/523-6379, 517/723-4677 (fax), www.emerypratt.com.

Ingram Book Company, One Ingram Blvd., P.O. Box 3006, La Vergne, TN 37086-1986, 615/213-5644, 615/213-5478, 800/937-8222 (phone), www.ipage.ingrambook.com, rob.riccuiti@ingrambook.com (Rob Ricciuti, Buyer).

Bookstores, etc.

www.Amazon.com, info@amazon.com, 800/201-7575 (phone), 206/266-2950 (fax).

Barnes & Noble and B. Dalton Books, 122 Fifth Avenue, New York, NY 10011, 212/633-3549, 866/873-2348, www.bn.com, dsimowski@bn.com.

Borders Group, Inc., 100 Phoenix Drive, Ann Arbor, MI 48108, 800/201-7575, www.borders.com, www.bordersstores.com (locations), (Scott White, Mgr. – 734/477-1851).

Walden Books, 100 Phoenix Drive, Ann Arbor, MI 48108, 800/322-2000, www.preferredreader.com.

The Latest Thing, 270 East 17th Street, Costa Mesa, CA 92627, 949/645-6211 (phone), 949/645-6210 (phone), 949/645-6461 (fax), www.latestthing.com.

Xlibris, 436 Walnut Street, 11th Floor, Philadelphia, PA 19106-3703, 888/795-4274 (phone), 215/923-4685 (fax), www.xlibris.com, john.fidler@xlibris.com.

eNovel, LLC, 4480 Springfield Road, Glen Allen, VA 23060, 804/783-0621 (phone), 804/783-0643 (fax), www.enovel.com, sales@enovel.com, Jack@enovel.com.

Libraries:

Orange County Public Library (29 branches), Administrative Headquarters: 714/566-3000; www.ocpl.org.

Los Angeles County Public Library (82 branches), 562/940-8534, www.colapublib.org, phyllisy@colapl.org.

Orange County City Branch Libraries (14); including Anaheim (4) at 714/765-3625, www.anaheim.net.comm_svc/apl/index.htm; Buena Park at 714/826-4100, www.buenapark.lib.ca.us; Fullerton (2) at 714/738-6326, www.ci.fullerton.ca.us/library; Huntington Beach at 714/842-4481, www.hbpl.org; Mission Viejo at 949/830-7100, www.cmvl.org; Newport Beach at 949/717-3828, www.newportbeachlibrary.org; Orange at 714/288-2471, www.library.cityoforange.org; Placentia at 714/528-1906, www.placentia.library.org; Santa Ana at 714/647-5250, www.youseemore.com; Yorba Linda at 714/777-2873, www.yorbalindalibrary.com.

H.W. Wilson Company, 950 University Avenue, Bronx, NY 10452, 718/588-8400, www.hwwilson.com, custserv@hwwilson.com.

Eastern Michigan University, 955 West Circle Drive, Ypsilanti, MI 48197, 734/487-0020, www.wemich.edu/hale.

Additionally, author is accessible through Books in Print (BIP), www.booksinprint.com and Bowkerlink, www.bowkerlink.com and various on-line websites. Her book has been deposited with the Library of Congress (LCCN 00-092018) and U.S. Copyright Office (TXu 953-633).

RECORD ALBUM

God's Love has been included as a song on HillTop Records'
<u>In the Beginning</u> album released March 2002.

HillTop Records
1777 No. Vine Street, Suite 411
Hollywood, CA 90028
In the Beginning, Order No. IB-116

DISSOCIATION MEETING

If you are interested in attending a dissociation meeting in
Orange County, California, e-mail author at
<u>writejuliem@jmmiraclesystempress.com</u>.

SECOND BOOK AVAILABLE
EARLY 2003

Facing Reality; ISBN 0-9702723-1-6.